Creative Mischief

Creative Mischief

Published by
LOAF Marketing Ltd
388 Strand
London WC2R 0LT
Tel ++44 (0)207 212 9940
www.loafmarketing.co.uk

All enquiries david@loafmarketing.co.uk

First edition 2009
Second edition 2011
Third edition 2013
Copyright © Dave Trott 2009, 2011. 2013

Printed in the European Union

A CIP catalogue record for this book is available from the
British Library.

ISBN - 978-0-9564357-0-5

Creative Mischief

DAVE TROTT

CONTENTS

INTRODUCTION

For me there are two requirements from anything I read.

I have to learn something.

Or I have to be entertained.

If I'm not getting either of those two, why would I keep reading?

The best advertising works because it's creative.

We can find creativity everywhere.

And we can all learn from it wherever we find it.

I can learn lessons about creativity from Mohammed Ali, Mike Tyson, Max Baer, Vince Lombardi, Billy Beane, Brian Clough, Tony Adams, Jackie Stewart, Bill Shankley, Ellen MacArthur, Napoleon Bonaparte, Horatio Nelson, Heinz Guderian, Michael Wittmann, Willy Messerschmitt, Woody Allen, George Carlin, Jackie Mason, Jo Brand, Rupert Murdoch, Richard Branson, Winston Churchill, Norman Tebbitt, Tony Benn, Pablo Picasso, Damien Hirst, Tintoretto, Orson Welles, Alfred Hitchcock, Emma Thompson, Clint Eastwood, Steven Spielberg, William of Ockham, Mary Wollstonecraft, Jean Paul Sartre, and Ernie Bilko.

All of these guys said or did something that made me go, "Wow, I wish I'd thought of that."

Just look at the cover of the Sergeant Pepper album.

That's The Beatles putting all their creative influences in one photograph.

And that was something I pored over at art school.

Why did they like all those people?

What was good about them?

I wanted to know what I could learn from them.

Whatever excites us will probably be something really clever.

It'll be good to read.

Although advertising can be very creative, it isn't the only form
of creativity.

It's applied creativity.

And there are lots of other forms of applied creativity.

So where else can we find it being applied?

What else took our breath away when we heard or saw it?

And what can we learn from it?

What can we take away and use?

Join up the dots. ■

CREATIVE MISCHIEF

There's a narrow line between humour and cruelty.

As creatives, a lot of what we do rides on that edge.

To be noticed, we need to do something different.

To be different, we need to break the rules.

To get away with breaking the rules, we need to be clever.

There it is.

We're always trying to get away with something.

To sail as close to the wind as we can without capsizing.

For instance:

Castlemaine lager's campaign, 'Australians wouldn't give a XXXX for any other lager'.

The poster campaign for French Connection UK:

FCUK FASHION and FCUK ADVERTISING.

The shop in the King's Road that sold brass front-door fittings, called Knobs and Knockers.

The Sun's headline when Tammy Wynette died,

COUNTRY STAR TAMMY: D-E-C-E-A-S-E-D.

Eddie Izzard's joke, "I come from a very traditional family. My grandad hanged himself on Christmas Eve and we couldn't take him down until January 5th."

This is a naughty, schoolboy, playground sense of humour.

It could explain why men outnumber women in creative departments.

It puts laughter above niceness. In the creative department, you can get away with anything, as long as it's funny.

When I worked at BMP, the Head of Television commuted in from Brighton every day.

He started reading The Exorcist on the train.

He said he thought it was the most evil book he'd ever read.

In fact, he said it was so evil he couldn't finish it.

So, at the weekend, he went to the end of Brighton pier and threw it as far as he could.

So I went to the bookshop.

I bought another copy.

Then I ran it under the tap.

And left it in his desk drawer.

For him to find.

As Dawn French says, "If it's funny it's not bad taste.

And if it's bad taste it's not funny." ■

ALL YOU'VE GOT TO BEAT IS YOURSELF

There's a great metaphor for life at the end of 'The Wizard of Oz'.

Dorothy, her dog Toto, the Tin Man, the Straw Man, and the

Cowardly Lion, spend the whole movie looking for The Wizard.

Oz is apparently so terrifying that everyone is scared stiff at the

mere mention of his name.

Finally, Dorothy manages to get an audience with Oz himself.

She and her companions are ushered into his presence.

They stand trembling.

The massive figure, forty feet high, wreathed in smoke, addresses

them in a booming voice.

"WHO DARES TO SEEK AN AUDIENCE WITH THE GREAT OZ?"

They can barely speak from fear.

Everything they've heard is true.

They are awe-struck.

But Dorothy's little dog Toto doesn't know any of this of course.

Because dogs can't talk.

So he hasn't been terrified by everything everyone's told them.

He just scampers across the room and pulls some curtains apart.

Behind the curtains is a little old man.

He is working levers and talking into a microphone.

The forty foot high Oz is actually just a mechanical device.

This little man within is working it like a machine.

They ask him why he did it.

He says it's because no one would take him seriously otherwise.

But people are impressed by size, so this way he gets attention.

Put simply, he lets people's minds do the work for him.

He lets their own minds create the stereotype they need to be frightened of.

They then live their lives in fear of the stereotype they themselves created.

That's what I was like before I went to New York.

I grew up in a reality with a set of rules I never questioned.

New York lifted me up out of that, and showed me my life from another angle.

New York was the little dog pulling the curtains apart.

Suddenly I could question all the things I'd thought were unquestionable.

What seemed to be facts were only true if I subscribed to it being that way.

I found that very empowering when I came back to London.

Powerful, important people weren't as frightening as I previously thought they were.

The things I'd been frightened of didn't exist in the real world.

Just in my head.

That was a more empowering lesson for me than anything I ever learned about advertising.

I see students and young people all the time trying to learn the rules, so they can follow them.

Trying to learn what they are, and aren't, allowed to do.

And then, later on, grumbling about the rules.

They learn the restrictions.

And then they enforce the restrictions on themselves.

And then grumble about it.

Of course we have to learn the rules.

Just as we would learn the rules of any game we were playing:
football, cricket, tennis.

But the rules are meant to be a springboard, not a straitjacket.

The floor, not the ceiling.

How can we ignore, or break, the rules and get away with it?

No one can teach you that.

You have to learn it for yourself. ■

CREATIVE ACCOUNT HANDLING

I don't think creativity belongs only in the so-called creative department.

In fact, that's often the least creative place.

As Edward de Bono said, "There are lots of people calling themselves creative who are actually mere stylists."

Creativity isn't a particular discipline.

It's the quality of originality and unexpectedness that you bring to whatever you do.

So what forms can creativity take in other departments?

In Kung Fu they have an expression, 'Wu Wei', translated as 'action by inaction'.

(Meaning, if possible it's always better to get your desired result by doing as little as possible.)

Amanda Walsh used to be our CEO and head suit (or frock).

One day she got a call from a new business prospect asking if we could help them sort out their strategy.

It was an obvious carrot for us.

If we helped them sort out their strategy, they'd issue it as the brief for a pitch and we'd be on the pitch list.

They asked us because they knew we had Murray Chick as a partner, one of the best strategists in town.

For me, this was a great chance to get an unfair advantage over the competition.

If I got Murray's strategy before the other agencies, then our creative department could start work earlier.

A bit like starting a race before the other competitors.

So I kept pestering Amanda and Murray:

Me (week one):   "Is the brief ready yet?"

Amanda: "Not yet, the client hasn't had a chance
to read it."

Me (week two):   "Hey, is the brief ready yet?"

Amanda: "Not yet. The client's still thinking about it."

Me (week three):   "Where the fuck is the brief?"

Amanda: "The client still hasn't made up their mind."

Me (week four):   "You've just wasted four weeks when we
could have been working on the pitch."

Amanda: "Look, calm down Dave.

We're not hassling the client because, while
they're dragging their feet they're running out
of time.

The whole process has gone on so long
that that they'll suddenly realise they're
about to miss their airdate.

They won't have time for a pitch and they'll
have to give us the account without one."

And that's exactly what happened.

Wu wei. ◼

CREATIVE SILENCE

I was talking to Helen Calcraft, Chief Exec of MCBD, about
making speeches.

I said I could relax and enjoy making a speech once I heard the
audience laughing.

Helen said she felt the opposite.

She had trained as an actor.

She felt she really had her audience when they were silent.

I'd never thought of it before, but it made perfect sense.

To her, silence was like white space to an art director.

It created room around what she was saying.

So there was nothing to distract from what she wanted you to
pay attention to.

For her, silence was clearing a space.

Brilliant.

Have you ever had that?

When someone tells you the opposite of what you've always
thought but it makes perfect sense?

The philosopher and mathematician Alfred North Whitehead said,
"Sometimes the opposite of a great truth is another great truth."

One of the most important creative uses of silence changed the
course of history.

It was in 1940, during the Second World War.

France was about to fall to the Germans, and Neville Chamberlain
was about to resign as Prime Minister of Great Britain.

He called Winston Churchill and Lord Halifax into his office.

He said, "Well, one of you two will have to replace me. Who's it going to be?"

Churchill wrote, "I knew no Englishman could ever say 'Give it to me'. So whoever spoke first would be the loser.

It was the longest 30 seconds of my life, but nothing would induce me to speak."

Eventually Halifax couldn't bear it any longer.

He cracked.

He said, "Well, I suppose you'd better give it to Winston."

Churchill accepted, and became Prime Minister.

Imagine the course of history if Churchill had spoken first.

Less is more. ■

CREATIVE EDITING

Someone recently said I persistently 'conflate' separate points to
make an argument.

I looked up 'conflate' in the dictionary and it says, "to fuse or bring
together separate elements".

I thought this was called 'creativity'.

Putting two unexpected things together, causing you to think about
them in a new way?

Isn't this a gorilla playing the drums?

Or a car made out of cake?

Or evolution going backwards?

Or waves morphing into white horses?

Conflation, in the modern creative sense, began with the Russian
director Eisenstein.

Previously the style of the American director D.W. Griffith had
dictated how films were edited.

This was strictly straight-line narrative:

Cut to man standing next to horse.

Cut to man taking horse's reins.

Cut to man's foot in stirrup.

Cut to man mounting horse.

Cut to horse disappearing into distance.

Eisenstein changed that.

He put together two disparate things, to create a third, wholly
unexpected, effect.

It didn't tell you the story in a linear form.

It made you feel the mood of what was happening:

Cut to Cossacks marching down steps.

Cut to old man collapsing.

Cut to Cossacks boots.

Cut to pram and baby falling down steps.

Cut to Cossacks rifles with bayonets.

Cut to nanny's screaming face.

This is the type of film-making that influenced European 'new wave' cinema, directors like Godard and Truffaut.

In turn, they influenced American cinema, directors like Martin Scorsese and Dennis Hopper.

Today we use it everywhere.

To suggest rather than define, what we want people to feel.

Conflation is another word for creativity.

The whole should be greater than the sum of the parts. ■

PREDATORY THINKING

Every football manager finds out everything they can about the opposition before they play them.

That way they can make sure their team knows how to take advantage of the other team's weaknesses.

That's predatory thinking.

Don Revie was a football manager who went further than that.

He built up a dossier on every referee in the league.

Then he found out which one would be in charge of that weekend's game.

Then he made each of his players study the referee's file.

So they knew the names of his family, where he'd been on holiday, what his hobbies were.

Just little things they could drop into the conversation in the tunnel, while waiting to go onto the pitch.

The referee would think they were nicer guys than the other team, who didn't know anything about him.

The usual statistics for refereeing decisions is roughly 50/50.

Half in your favour, half against.

But over the season Leeds got over 70% of decisions in their favour, and under 30% against.

Under Don Revie, Leeds won 3 championships, 3 cups, and 2 EUFA Cups.

That's real predatory thinking.

If you want something, you have to take it off someone else.

You have to out-think them.

There's the story of two explorers walking through the jungle.

Suddenly they hear a tiger roar.

One explorer sits down and takes a pair of running shoes out of his back pack.

"You're crazy, you'll never outrun a tiger," says the other explorer.

"I don't have to outrun the tiger," he replies.

"I just have to outrun you."

Conventional thinking is that the best man wins.

That's also lazy thinking.

How do you beat someone who's better than you?

That's creative thinking.

As Maurice Saatchi used to say,

"I don't have to win. I just have to make you lose." ■

DESIRE AND PERMISSION

How does advertising work?

It works the same way as every other purchase decision.

Every purchase decision is a combination of 'desire' and 'permission'.

Without those two elements nothing happens.

If you want to buy something, but you can't justify it in any way, you don't buy it.

If you can justify buying something, but you don't want it, you don't buy it.

It's that simple.

You've got to want something, and it's got be okay for you to have it.

The 'desire' part is the right brain: the emotional part.

The 'permission' part is the left brain: the rational part.

The emotional side of your brain wants it.

The rational side of your brain says whether you can have it.

Think of the traditional car ad.

Big beautiful shot of a sexy looking car on the left hand page.

All the statistics on the right hand page (5 bearing crankshaft, 16 valve engine, double overhead-camshafts, ABS, SIPS, etc., etc.)

What makes your emotional side want the car is the big, beautiful photo.

But your rational side won't let you buy a car just on what it looks like.

So your rational side has to be reassured by the statistics on the other page.

Without the beautiful photo, your emotional side wouldn't want the car.

Without the statistics as evidence, your rational side wouldn't be happy to part with the money.

Now because not every purchase decision costs as much as a car, it's not always as obvious as that.

It might be much more subtle and sophisticated.

But with everything, from a chocolate bar to perfume, there has to be desire, and there has to be permission.

And that's not just true of advertising.

That's true of every single decision you make in your life.

From the day you're born until the day you die.

Desire, permission.

Advertising is the same as everything else. ■

ETHNIC HUMOUR

It's difficult to be a writer in a foreign country.

An example happened to me last week.

I was at Hampstead tube, and the ticket collector had a new walkie-talkie.

He was obviously very proud of it.

He spoke into it loudly enough for us all to hear.

He said:

"Tango 1 calling Tango 2.

Tango 1 calling Tango 2.

Over."

I heard a muffled voice reply something.

Then the ticket collector said testily into it:

"No Chris: you're Tango 3, Terry's Tango 2."

I laughed to myself, and thought something that silly could only happen in this country.

It makes you proud to be British.

Then I thought, why is that?

Why are we so proud of looking silly?

Germans or Spanish or Chinese would die before they'd let anyone see them looking silly.

We revel in it.

Take the war in Afghanistan.

The British and American forces were involved in really heavy fighting with the Taliban.

The worst of the fighting was in and around the caves of Tora Bora.

The American forces dubbed them, 'The Caves of Death'.

The British forces referred to them as, 'Tora Bora Tomkinson'.

Later I read a report about the airborne tanker crews.

The American pilots were flying missions from carriers in The Gulf.

They didn't have enough fuel to make the return trip unless they refuelled at night, 30,000 feet up, from British airborne tankers.

One American pilot said, "These guys flew missions that saved our lives.

But when we linked up with them, they held signs up to the window saying, 'CASH ONLY, NO CHEQUES'. I don't know, is that your humour?"

The same thing happened in World War 2.

It was 1940 and America wasn't in the war.

France had just fallen and everyone knew Britain was next.

Ed Murrow, the famous American reporter, was doing a weekly radio broadcast back to the US from London.

He said, "Sometimes it's hard for an American to understand the British. Today the whole of Europe has fallen to Nazi Germany. Only the people of this small island are left, on their own against a mighty war machine. And yet as I went on the street this morning, the mood of the population seemed somehow lighter, more optimistic. It didn't make any sense. Then I saw a newspaper seller with a placard in front of him that read,

'BRITAIN AND GERMANY IN THE FINAL'." ■

THE SPOKEN WORD vs THE PRINTED WORD

A couple of years back, Radio 4 ran a programme on the history
of swearing and how it started.

Apparently it was the Victorians who invented the concept.

It didn't exist before them.

The words existed of course.

But not the concept that some words were unfit for use.

What caused the invention of swearing was the advent of road signs.

With the Victorians came the need to formalise every address.

So they could supply sewage to every house, gas or electric,
mail delivery, everything we now take for granted.

The problem was London had grown organically over two
thousand years.

Streets just happened to be pathways between groups of houses.

They acquired nicknames that were just a way to describe them.

So you might tell someone to go to, "The street with all
the blacksmiths".

This would pretty soon be shortened to 'Blacksmith Street'.

Which is how we got 'Butcher Street' or 'Baker Street' or
'Leather Lane'.

So far so good.

But the problem was slang.

For instance, a street of stables might be known as 'Horseshit Row'.

Because that was its most noticeable feature.

The BBC said one alley, that prostitutes used, was known as

'Grope Cunt Lane'.

Before the advent of road signs this wasn't a problem.

Polite Victorian society wouldn't have any reason to talk about these streets, much less walk down them.

But suddenly every street was going to have its named printed in large black and white letters.

Up where everyone could see it.

'GROPE CUNT LANE' just wasn't going to happen.

So a lot of streets had to be renamed.

And a list of unfit words was compiled.

And the concept of swearing was born.

Grope Cunt Lane, for instance, had to be renamed as 'Grape Lane'.

The main point being, when you see something written down it has a much more 'in your face' quality than something merely spoken.

When John Major was Prime Minister he knew his own party were against him, and called them "a bunch of shits".

The next day, Sue Douglas, editor of The Sunday Express, ran that as the front-page headline: 'BUNCH OF SHITS'.

She was fired.

Somehow it was much more powerful to see it, than just to hear it.

The same is true in advertising.

Nick Wray once wrote a very nice commercial for Mazda.

The commercial took place in a massive warehouse.

Huge wooden boxes were lifted, one-at-a-time, to reveal smaller boxes underneath, like Russian dolls.

It went roughly like this:

(A huge wooden box is lifted by chains, revealing a slightly smaller second box.)

Announcer: "The outside of a Rolls Royce is bigger than the outside of a Mazda."

(The second wooden box is lifted, revealing a third wooden box.)

Announcer: "But the inside of a Mazda…"

(The third wooden box is lifted, revealing an even smaller fourth wooden box.)

Announcer: "… is bigger than the inside of a Rolls Royce."

Voice: "That's amazing."

(Dissolve through to Mazda logo.)

Announcer: "No, that's a Mazda."

The problem was we couldn't print the words 'Rolls Royce' on the box.
If we showed the name it was considered copyright infringement.
Whereas if we merely said it, it wasn't.
Which was a shame.

Because, although the ad was a strong demonstration of a good fact, it would have been simpler, more powerful, and more memorable to have the words 'Rolls Royce' and 'Mazda' on the boxes.

A picture may not always be worth a thousand words, but to see something is often more emphatic than just hearing it. ■

UNIVERSITY vs ART SCHOOL

Personally, I tend to find that the more you live in the academic world, the less you live in the real world.

I suppose it has to be that way really.

Being able to write a paper about something is, in that world, more important than actually doing something.

After all, the person who actually did it might not know why they did it.

It might have been an accident.

But if you can analyse it, debate it, argue it, you must have truly understood it.

(Which is why creatives might find planners patronising.)

Anyway, university is a little world unto itself, it's a closed loop.

Ergo, the more illustrious your university career, the further you recede from the world the rest of us inhabit.

This was illustrated to me once by a young account man (names don't matter, do they Seb?).

He had, apparently, a very fine mind, and an honours degree.

He sent down a brief for the creative department, for me to sign off.

It was the launch of a new product.

The part I'll always remember is his final sentence:

"For details of pack artwork, see attached reference."

I turned the page and there in the middle of it was a one-inch black square.

Nothing else, just a black square.

I called him down and asked if we could discuss his brief.

When he came in he asked if I had a problem with the strategy.

I said, "No, not the strategy."

He said, "Only I've heard emotional and affinity strategies always seem to vex you."

I said, "I bet you went to a really good university didn't you?"

He smiled and said, "Yes I did. Cambridge as a matter of fact, how did you know?"

I held up the page with the single black square on it and said, "Because, you twat, you've Xeroxed a 35mm slide."

As Napoleon said,

"Generals don't win wars. Sergeants win wars." ■

BEING RIGHT vs BEING INTERESTING

I always tell students they will usually have to make a choice.

On the one hand: being right, but dull.

On the other hand: being wrong, but interesting.

So which should they choose?

I say go for interesting every time.

Why doesn't most advertising work?

Because it's 'right'.

It's been debated, discussed, argued, briefed, researched, debriefed, rebriefed, until it's 'right'.

And that's the problem: it's right.

It's not interesting.

It's not interesting, so no one notices it.

No one notices it so no one remembers it.

No one remembers it so it doesn't work.

No matter how 'right' it is.

There is just too much advertising out there for all of it to work.

Statistics say we are each exposed to roughly 1,000 different advertising messages a day.

How many do you remember from yesterday?

Radio, posters, tube cards, online pop-ups, SMS, ambient, TV, magazine ads, newspaper ads, viral ads.

You can probably remember one that was really good.

And one that was really bad.

The extremes.

Because extremes are interesting.

They're interesting because they haven't had all the life sucked out of them by being made right.

Visibility isn't about being right.

It's about being interesting.

As Picasso said, "What use are computers? All they can do is give you answers."

A women doesn't really want Mr. Right.

She wants Mr. Interesting.

In the pub, who do you want to listen to?

The bloke who's always right?

Or the bloke who's always interesting?

Being right is overrated.

Because being right is seen as the truth.

But what is the truth?

The truth is whatever you believe it is.

And you only believe what you want to believe.

And you only want to believe what's interesting.

As Churchill said, "Never let the truth spoil a good story." ■

CHANGE THE RULES

When Mohammed Ali was young he was known as Cassius Clay.

He was also known as 'The Louisville Lip' because of his arrogance.

He would predict, in rhyme, the round he'd knock his opponents out.

"I'm wise to his tricks,

so he must fall in round six.

But if he talks in jive,

I'll put him down in five."

At first everyone laughed at the arrogance of such a loud mouth.

But boxers started to fall in the rounds he predicted.

And pretty soon everyone stopped laughing.

This was something no one had seen before.

A man who was so supremely self-confident it wasn't even a question of whether he'd win, just what round.

Other boxers were terrified.

The question came to be not, would they lose, but could they survive the round Clay had predicted.

They became so terrified of the accuracy of his predictions, defeat seemed almost inevitable.

His opponents' confidence evaporated.

They were beaten and demoralised before they started.

Years later he admitted that his early opponents weren't that impressive.

So, to make himself stand out, he would predict a round to win.

Often he could have knocked them out in the first round.

But he waited, and kept the fight going, until the round he predicted.

Because he knew it would have a greater effect on the better

fighters who were watching.

The ones he'd have to fight next.

So he changed the rules of the game.

Frank Lowe did something similar.

As CEO of Collett Dickenson Pearce, he asked Mike Yershon,

the head of media, to buy every 48 sheet poster within a mile

radius of the agency.

Then he made sure that all CDP's clients' posters ran on them.

So that any new business client coming in to see CDP

would have seen all their advertising before they even got

to the agency.

And when Frank Lowe showed them the agency's work, they were

impressed that everything seemed like famous campaigns.

Because, without realising it, they'd just seen everything on posters,

on the way there.

Like Cassius Clay, Frank had won the game before it even started. ■

CONTEXT IS EVERYTHING

Mark Twain tells the story of a young boy he met in the mid-West.

Every time a stranger came into town the other boys delighted in showing the stranger just how stupid this boy was.

They'd hold out two coins, a dime (10 cents) and a nickel (5 cents), and tell the boy he could keep one.

He'd always pick the nickel because it was bigger.

Every time he did it all the other boys laughed.

Mark Twain took him aside and said, "Son, I have to tell you that the small coin is worth more than the bigger one."

The boy said, "I know that mister. But how many times do you think they'd let me choose if I picked the more valuable one?"

In the original context, the boy is stupid.

Change the context, and he's smart.

This is what the government of Singapore did.

Singapore is a small island, and short of organs for transplants.

Like Britain, people are too lazy to carry an organ donor card.

So the Singapore government changed the law.

Everyone's organs are automatically donated when they die.

Unless they carry a non-donor card.

Now Singapore has plenty of organs for transplants.

Because everyone's too lazy to carry a non-donor card.

In the original context laziness was a problem.

Change the context and laziness solves the problem.

It works in advertising too.

London Docklands was an inner city development area.

Dockland's main competitor was Milton Keynes.

It was portrayed in the ads as a pretty place to live, lots of green fields, cows and sheep, out in the country.

Docklands looked like an awful place to live by comparison.

So we changed the context.

Instead of looking for a great place to LIVE, you should be looking for a great place to WORK.

Paul Grubb and Steve Henry wrote the strapline,

'WHY MOVE TO THE MIDDLE OF NOWHERE, WHEN YOU CAN MOVE TO THE MIDDLE OF LONDON'.

By changing the context, moving a business to the country looked like a dumb thing to do.

It worked so well that Docklands now has the tallest buildings in Europe, and Milton Keynes still has green fields and cows.

And, of course, it's true for media.

Roughly the same amount of people with money used to read The News of the World and The Sunday Times.

So, where would you have put an ad for Rolex?

Think what the media says about the brand.

It's not just about the ad, it's about where it runs.

Like everything, it's all about context. ■

CONTEXT ISN'T EVERYTHING, IT'S THE ONLY THING

A couple of years ago I went to a Caravaggio exhibition at The National Gallery in Trafalgar Square.

One of the greatest painters ever, it was always going to be packed.

In fact so many people wanted to see it that you had to book a ticket, just like a show at the cinema or theatre.

You booked a particular time, then you went along and queued with everyone else.

Even then, when we got inside the exhibition it was packed.

It was in the basement, and just coming down the stairs you could see the crowd already. It was almost impossible to get near any of the pictures.

The star picture of the whole show was 'Supper at Emmaus' showing Christ seated with three people.

The crowd around this particular painting was about six or seven deep.

I don't think anyone could have enjoyed it or studied it, or spent more than a few minutes in front of it.

The crowd was like a single jostling mass, and you had to move with it.

I didn't even bother trying to see that particular Caravaggio.

There wasn't any point.

All year round it's on show upstairs in the main part of The National Gallery.

You can go to see it for free any time you want.

You can have the whole painting to yourself because hardly anyone goes to look at it.

I knew this because, when my children were small, they'd asked me how to draw something to look like it's coming towards you when it's on a flat piece of paper.

I knew a guy called Alan Reid, who was a bit of an art expert.

So I asked him where I could find some good examples of 'foreshortening'.

He said the best example was 'Supper at Emmaus' which hung at The National.

So we went along on a Saturday, sat on the floor in front of it, and spent a peaceful hour or so drawing it.

We had it to ourselves because no one had directed anyone's attention to it.

But as soon as it's in an exhibition downstairs, you can't get near it for the crowds. Isn't that an amazing thing?

We seem incapable of judging for ourselves what's good, we need someone to tell us.

If it's just hanging in a gallery with no one looking at it, how can it be any good? But if it's in a major exhibition, it must be important and we need to see it.

In Singapore they have an expression for this sort of herd behaviour. It's called 'Kia Soo'.

Loosely translated as 'fear of being left out'.

Like seeing a crowd, and rushing over to see what everyone's looking at in case you missed something.

I saw an exhibition once at The Saatchi Gallery.

One piece that fascinated me was by Gavin Turk.

It was a piece of used chewing gum inside a glass case.

It wasn't the piece itself that fascinated me.

For me the real art was watching the people gathered around the case studying a piece of used chewing gum.

They must have passed dozens of identical pieces of gum on the way to the gallery.

Probably they'd pass dozens more on the way home.

Would they stop and study each one?

Would they stroke their chin and ponder on the meaning?

Of course not.

They wouldn't even see them, and even if they did they wouldn't be worth discussing, admiring, studying, emulating.

See we don't judge the object for ourselves.

We judge the fact that someone else says it has merit.

And we don't want to be left out ('Kia Soo').

But art galleries shouldn't be like rubber stamps.

They should be fun and provocative, they should stimulate your mind, not close it down.

They're an opinion, not an authority.

Just like advertising awards. ■

POSITIONING

Once you've read absolutely every single word of George Lois's book 'The Art of Advertising', there is only one other advertising book I usually recommend.

This book isn't so creative as George Lois's.

It's not so inspirational.

But it is simple, and clever, and powerful.

'Positioning: The Battle for your Mind' by Al Ries and Jack Trout.

Like George Lois's book, I can't do it justice in a couple of paragraphs.

But 'positioning' shows you how to get a hook in the consumer's consciousness.

And that's very different to what everyone thinks our job is.

Most people think our job is to make the consumer like the brand.

Which is why 90% of advertising (£17 billion in the UK alone) doesn't work.

What's actually much more important is what makes the brand different.

If you aren't different, you have no identity.

You're just a commodity.

Just a manufacturer in fact, you have no brand.

So to have a brand you need an identity.

To have an identity you need a point of difference.

And if you don't have one, you need to create one.

For example, supposing I asked the question, who was the first American President?

Most people would be able to answer, George Washington.

But if I asked, who was the forty-fourth American President, a lot less people would be able to answer.

You can't remember all the American Presidents, and what order they came in.

Why would you?

You can certainly remember the names of a few American Presidents: Lincoln, Roosevelt, Kennedy, Nixon, Bush.

But who cares what number they were?

So, no, most people don't know, and can't be bothered, who was the forty-fourth American President.

Now suppose I asked, who was the first black American President?

Everyone would answer, Barack Obama.

You know that immediately because he has a definite point of difference.

So he stands out.

Actually, Barack Obama is also the forty-fourth President.

But no one remembers that.

Because that positioning has no point of difference.

As a number, he's just one of forty four.

But as a black President, he is one of one.

And that's a powerful position.

That's a brand. ■

NEVER MIND THE BRAND BOLLOCKS

In the late sixties I'd just started at art school in Brooklyn.

I was really disappointed.

Everyone was so uncool.

They either dressed like slobs or nerds.

I'd just come from London, I was a mod.

I thought if London was stylish, New York would be way more so.

But I was wrong.

Style had totally bypassed America.

They thought if you were stylish you must be gay.

So most of the other students ignored me.

This wasn't the rebellious, outrageous, art school atmosphere
I'd been expecting.

I felt like I'd been exiled to an old folk's home.

Then one day I was walking across campus and this blonde guy
came up and asked me where I got my hair cut.

He was from Queens, and he sounded like Yogi Bear when he talked.

He liked my hair because it didn't look like anyone else's.

I told him I cut it myself.

He asked me if I'd cut his, so I said yeah.

And we became friends.

He didn't want to be like everyone else either.

He wanted to be different.

He didn't even like wearing the same clothes as everyone else.

So he used to buy all his clothes from thrift shops (the NYC
equivalent of Oxfam shops).

But not just for cheapness, for weirdness.

He would buy things you couldn't find anywhere else.

White hob-nailed construction boots, WW2 floor length army greatcoats, sequin-covered trapeze artist's leotards.

Stuff like that.

We shared a student flat for a few years.

Gradually the sixties turned into the seventies and we both went different ways.

I came back to London to work in advertising.

He stayed in New York and founded a group, called The New York Dolls.

His name was Artie Kane and he was the bass player.

They were quite successful for a while.

But not because of their music.

Because of their style, or lack of it: their couldn't-give-a-fuckness.

They were a brand not a product.

They came to the UK and visited Vivienne Westwood's bondage shop.

Malcolm MacLaren saw them and became their manager for a while.

He said it was the first time he realised you didn't have to be able to play a note to be rock stars.

It was all about image.

All about the pose.

Eventually he found four other teenagers hanging around the shop and formed the Sex Pistols.

And punk was born.

A marketing vision that was much more about brand (image) than product (music).

Maclaren understood that people buy a product for what it DOES.

But they buy a brand for what it SAYS about them.

People bought the New York Dolls (and afterwards punk) not for the high quality of the music.

They bought it for the rebellious image it gave them.

They bought it for the badge.

Being seen with the album cover said far more about you than listening to the record inside.

That's brand over product.

See, anyone can be a motorcycle rebel.

You don't have to drive a Harley Davidson.

You just have to wear a T-shirt with the Harley logo on.

Artie never did advertising, but he understood the power of a brand way before I did. ■

MAD MEN

A few months ago, I got a call from a TV producer.

They were about to start showing the series 'Mad Men', showing what advertising was like in the 60s in New York.

They wanted to put together a programme on David Ogilvy to show beforehand.

They wanted Ogilvy because he was a Brit, and worked his way up to become one of the giants of Madison Avenue.

She wanted to interview me for the show because I had been learning and working in advertising in New York at that time.

She wanted me to say how fabulous we all thought David Ogilvy was.

I told her I had a problem with that.

For me Ogilvy was a dinosaur.

He was the end of an era.

He represented what advertising used to be.

When advertisers patronised punters and told them,

"Wear a Hathaway shirt and you too can enter the romantic world of the man with the mysterious eye patch."

That's how advertising had always been.

Pretence, designed to fool the gullible.

No doubt Ogilvy was massively successful.

But New York advertising was split into two groups.

You were either Ogilvy or Bernbach.

Bernbach was starting a revolution.

Truth in advertising.

Don't tell people this shirt will fulfil your wildest fantasies, turn you into James Bond, make women fall at your feet, and make your boss give you a rise.

Tell them the actual advantages this shirt has over other shirts.

But only the truth.

And tell them in an amusing, memorable way.

And let them decide.

And don't just use perfect looking WASPs (White Anglo Saxon Protestants) in the advertising.

Don't tell everyone to aspire to something they can never be.

Use real people, Italians, Chinese, Jews, Blacks.

The people that actually lived in New York.

If you showed them in advertising they'd feel good about themselves.

Instead of feeling bad, and wishing they were something else.

For the first time, Bernbach showed everyone that advertising could be a force for good.

Instead of just a shoddy way to make money.

So, I said to the producer, if you want me to come on and talk about Bernbach, I will.

But of course, that wasn't the programme she had in mind. ■

THE LAZY MIND

I often talk about advertising that sells, and what we can learn from it to make our own advertising better.

There's always someone who responds with,

"Why are you always defending bad advertising?"

This is the equivalent of Churchill saying we need to learn Rommel's secrets in order to beat him.

And getting the response,

"Why are you always bigging-up the Nazis?"

This is the lazy mind.

The mind (not just yours or mine: everybody's) always defaults to the easy solution: the lazy solution.

This is because the mind is basically a pattern-making machine.

How the mind works is called 'Gestalt'.

There is way too much information all around us all the time.

The only way to deal with it all is to group it into large, distinct collections of similar stuff.

So for instance, you don't walk along the street analysing the difference in the hundreds of cars you see (make, colour, occupants, number plate, age, condition).

If you did, you'd never get to the end of the street.

You just have the broad grouping 'cars'.

And these broad-groupings (cars, houses, politics, food, shops, people, time) allow you to handle what would otherwise be a literally infinite amount of information.

So the mind is a pattern-making machine.

That's its job, and that's how it helps us survive.

That's what's good about it.

What's bad about it, is when we need it to delve a little
deeper into the patterns and actually notice the differences
on a subtler level.

The mind doesn't want to do that, that's not its job.

No one wants to re-invent the wheel every time.

That's way too much like hard work.

So let's just default to one of the broad groups: Good or Bad.

So left to itself, the mind can result in bigotry.

By grouping things, and never questioning the grouping.

(That red vehicle is a car. Cars are bad. Therefore that red vehicle
is bad. Without ever bothering to find out that the red vehicle
is actually a battery driven car, used by a paramedic to get
to emergencies.)

Delving into subtler differences isn't the mind's job.

The mind is too lazy for that, it just likes big, easy groups.

Orwell parodied this in Animal Farm.

'Four legs good. Two legs bad'.

That's how propaganda works: oversimplify.

But propaganda, like anything else, isn't necessarily bad.

It can be a force for good and, to an extent, it's what we do.

Understand how the mind works so that we can use it.

Because that's what we're dealing with.

Changing and motivating people's minds.

But before we can do anything with other people's minds,
we have to be able to control our own.

That means we have to investigate and question our own minds.

How does it work, and who's in charge.

It won't feel comfortable, because since we've been born we've learned to depend on our minds.

Probably, right now, your mind is telling you this is rubbish.

So you can switch off and stay with what you already know.

There's no possibility of growth unless you have an open mind.

That means investigating whatever's new before you make a decision about it.

The difference is between Scepticism and Cynicism.

Scepticism is where you say,

"I won't believe it until you prove it."

Cynicism is where you say,

"I won't believe it, even if you prove it."

All knowledge comes from Scepticism.

Ignorance and fear come from Cynicism.

So, when I talk about what we can learn from bad advertising, please be sceptical not cynical. ∎

REALLY CREATIVE PEOPLE

Simon Veksner (aka Scamp) made an interesting point about creative people.

He says, "I've noticed that the very best creatives don't tend to get bored, because they're the ones who are complete novelty whores, in other words they're the ones who are most easily bored/scared of boredom in the first place. If that makes any sense.

It also explains why they win so many awards.

New stuff wins awards."

I agree with him, really creative people are fascinated by 'new' stuff.

But that doesn't just mean the latest technology.

It means stuff that is new to them.

It might be a hundred years old, but they've never seen it before.

It might be an African sculpture, a Russian film, a shocking piece of grafitti, a graphic wine label, a strange chair.

The cleverness, for them, is in finding something original and unusual.

Paul Arden had a progressive lung disease.

For the last year of his life he couldn't leave his oxygen machine.

He had a tube running from it that allowed him to walk around the ground floor of his cottage.

My son and daughter called him up to say they were coming down to see him. (He and his wife, Toni, were their godparents).

He said, "Yes, but you can only come if you bring two new things each. And they mustn't be to do with advertising."

Even stuck in a cottage at the end of an oxygen tube he wanted stimulation.

He wanted to be surprised.

He wanted his own imagination triggered and his optimism for possibility fired.

He wanted the thrill that it hasn't all been done yet.

That there's still tons left to do out there, if only we'll look.

And it's not just waiting for Apple or Nokia to launch a new gimmick.

That's as creative as waiting for a train to come into the station, and being the first to jump on.

The point isn't in waiting for someone else to invent something new.

The point is in discovering something fresh and exciting yourself.

That's why the walls of John Webster's office were full of pieces of paper he'd torn out of books or magazines.

Illustrations, paintings, photographs he knew he'd use one day.

Magritte, Steinberg, Bert Hardy or, better yet, someone unknown.

Carl Ally was one of the great New York agencies.

Carl Ally himself used to say,

"The creative person wants to be a know-it-all. He wants to know about all kinds of things: ancient history, nineteenth century mathematics, current manufacturing techniques, flower arranging, and hog futures. He never knows when these ideas might come together to form a new idea. It may happen six minutes later, or six years down the road. But the creative person has faith that it will happen."

The funny thing I notice is that this naïve attitude, this openness, the child-like thrill of discovering new things seems to be more prevalent among art directors than copywriters.

Is it nature or nurture?

Do you learn that at art school?

Or do you go to art school because you're already like that?

Either way it's a much better way to go through life.

On a voyage of constant discovery.

That way you squeeze every drop out of your time on the planet.

Even at the very end Paul Arden still wanted to know what's new.

What hadn't he seen yet. ■

IF YOU'RE CREATIVE, CREATE

I hear people complaining that there are no opportunities.

That no one will give them a chance.

That there's no way out of their situation.

There's nothing they can do and it's not their fault.

Here's a thing.

There have never been any opportunities.

No one was ever feeling sorry for themselves, when someone knocked on the door and said, "How would you like me to show you a way out of this?"

It doesn't happen like that.

Never has, never will.

That's like sitting around waiting to win the lottery.

It's about hope.

And hope is putting the problem in someone else's hands.

Hope isn't very creative.

Robert Campbell and Mark Roalfe were a young creative team.

They had a job at an agency they weren't happy at.

They wanted something better.

So what could they do?

Either leave the job, and the money, and take a big chance.

Then if they can't get a job, wish they'd never left.

Or stay where they are, and hope someone knocks on the door with a better job offer.

Neither of those were good options.

So because they were creative, they created another option.

They pretended they were students and got Andrew Cracknel, then creative director of WCRS, to offer them a two-week placement.

Then they took two weeks holiday from their job and, instead of going away, went to WCRS.

After the two week placement they reckoned they'd either have a job at WCRS, or at least still have their old job to fall back on.

How creative is that?

And how many people would have thought of it?

But that's what really creative people do.

Come up with an answer where everyone else says there isn't one.

They were so determined, they got the job at WCRS after two weeks.

Then they eventually went on to open their own agency.

It was called Rainey Kelly Campbell Roalfe, and they eventually sold it for a fortune to Y&R.

Mike Stephenson and Derek Apse were a young team at BMP.

Absolutely all creative work at BMP was researched.

Scripts were made into crude animatics to show to groups of housewives.

These animatics were done on the cheap.

So a lot of good scripts never made it through research.

Creative teams sat around and grumbled about how many good ideas they lost this way.

An atmosphere of negativity set in.

People stopped trying so hard because they knew they'd lose their best stuff in research.

This didn't make any sense to Mike and Derek.

They thought they should put the absolute maximum effort into making the animatics as good as possible.

That way, even if the script didn't get made, they'd have a great little film for their reel.

And that's what they did.

Absolutely every animatic they made was done with amost as much care and effort as a real commercial.

Little films that you could almost have run on TV.

They had such a great little reel, they used it to get a job at Lowe.

An agency where everything didn't get researched.

And they used everything they learned making animatics to get a lot of really good scripts made.

And eventually one of them became a creative director, and the other a film director.

They saw an opportunity where no one else could.

By turning a problem into an opportunity.

Opportunities aren't going to crop up.

You have to create them.

That's what being creative is. ■

FORM CAN BE EMOTIONAL FUNCTION

I started off at art school wanting to be a painter.

But my problem was the subjectivity of the whole thing.

How do you know if a painting's any good, who decides?

Van Gogh was treated as a fool in his lifetime, and died a pauper.

Never sold a painting to a gallery and couldn't get an exhibition.

Yet after he died the same paintings were suddenly considered genius and worth millions.

Who decides and how?

What are the rules?

Well, quite simply there aren't any.

Whether a painting is any good or not is decided by a small, influential, group of critics and gallery owners.

So, if you're a painter, their subjectivity decides your ability.

I didn't like this.

It was like playing football with no rules, and the referee deciding who he preferred, on whatever grounds he chose.

So, when I went to New York, I switched to advertising.

I decided that at least, that way, millions of ordinary people in the street would decide whether I was any good or not.

And, while I was there, I made friends with a lot of guys studying Industrial Design.

We talked a lot about what they did on their courses, and I learned a lot.

I thought what they did was a lot closer to advertising than painting was.

Painting was a one-off object designed to hang in galleries and be viewed, considered, pondered over, and interpreted by the cultural elite.

Industrial Design was in three dimensions, advertising was in two dimensions, but both were about the mass production of an idea.

Both had to be able to work in the real world, not just an art gallery.

Both had to be about cost, and return on investment.

Both would be judged by how they performed against measurable criteria, not just whether they pleased half a dozen critics.

I'd never heard of The Bauhaus before these guys told me about it.

But one particular Bauhaus maxim flipped the light switch on in my head.

FORM FOLLOWS FUNCTION.

The most important word being 'follows'.

Written in a less alliterative way, that would read,

"Every part of the eventual design must have a reason, or it shouldn't be there."

Suddenly, anyone could take any piece of design or advertising apart and analyse it.

I loved the anti-elitism of it.

I loved the way we could lift up the bonnet and demand to know why something was there, and what it did.

This became my mantra, and over the years I've never deviated from it.

Until...

One evening I was discussing this with the designer Richard Seymour.

He wasn't quite as black and white about it as I was.

He said to me, "Yes Dave, but form can be emotional function."

In other words, a pleasing shape can also fulfill a purpose.

Just by being pleasing.

I wasn't having it.

But, because of how much I respect Richard as a designer and a thinker, it stayed in my brain.

I know I can learn a lot about what I do, just from listening to him talk about what he does.

And then I found this extract from the diary of Lieutenant Colonel Mervin Willett Gonin DSO, a British colonel who was amongst the first to liberate a Nazi concentration camp in 1945.

> "It took a little time to get used to seeing men, women, and children collapse as you walked by them and to restrain oneself from going to their assistance.
>
> One had to get used early to the idea that the individual just did not count.
>
> It was shortly after the British Red Cross arrived, though it may have no connection, that a very large quantity of lipstick arrived. This was not at all what we men wanted, we were screaming for hundreds and thousands of other things: food and medical equipment, and I don't know who asked for lipstick. I wish so much that I could discover who did it; it was the action of genius, sheer unadulterated brilliance.

I believe nothing did more for those internees than the lipstick. Women lay in bed with no sheets and no nightie but with scarlet red lips, you saw them wandering about with nothing but a blanket over their shoulders, but with scarlet red lips.

I saw a woman dead on the post mortem table and clutched in her hand was a piece of lipstick. At last someone had done something to make them individuals again, they were someone, no longer merely the number tattooed on the arm.

At last they could take an interest in their appearance. That lipstick started to give them back their humanity."

And my world shifted a little bit.

It seems I was wrong.

Form can be emotional function. ■

DON'T LET ANYONE ELSE WRITE YOUR AGENDA

I was one of two deputy creative directors at BMP.

One day the managing director came to see me.

He said, "We've got a real problem with (the other deputy CD).

He never stops complaining about you to the entire board, and anyone else that will listen."

I said, "What sort of things does he say?"

The MD said, "He says you can't do your job.

That you're not as good as he is.

That nobody likes you, they'd all prefer to be working for him.

That you shouldn't be a deputy CD, he should be the only one."

I knew the MD was right.

I had found advertising annuals the other deputy CD had left on John Webster's desk, with Post-it notes reading,

"This is where Trott stole his latest TV idea from."

To be fair it was getting to be a bit of a drag.

So I thought about the problem for a bit.

Then I said to the MD, "Why don't you give him a raise?"

The MD said, "Why would we do that, he's making himself a pain in the arse?"

I said, "Yes, but John's not going to fire him for that is he?

And anyway, he's a good writer.

We just want to make the problem go away.

And the problem is that this guy sees me as direct competition.

Give him a raise so he's earning more than me.

Then he won't feel threatened by me.

That'll make the problem go away and I can get on with my work without the constant aggravation."

The MD said, "Wouldn't you mind if we gave him a raise and not you?"

I said, "Not really. What I earn compared to him is irrelevant to me.

If he earns more than me, it doesn't make my salary worth any less.

And if he earns less than me it doesn't make my salary worth any more.

I still get what I get.

It just gets him off my back."

And that's how it worked out.

As soon as the guy knew he was earning more than me he relaxed.

He was even quite patronizing towards me, as if he felt sorry for me.

Because he thought he'd won, and I'd lost.

But I didn't mind.

Because he never knew it was my idea.

And it solved the problem.

See he was a guy who was interested in rising inside BMP, and the only way he knew how to do that was by internal politics.

I was interested in building a career in advertising.

And I thought the only way to do that was through the work.

So internal politics didn't interest me.

I just wanted to do as much good work as I could get my hands on, as fast as I could.

Now, if I had let this guy get me angry, I might have started to play him at his own game.

I would have started bad mouthing him around the agency.

I would have tried to prove to John Webster that he was crap.

I would have had to play internal politics instead of concentrating on the work.

But the problem with playing his game is just that.

It's his game.

It's not mine.

And if it's his game, he must be better at it.

And why would I play a game I'm sure to lose at?

So I didn't let him write my agenda.

I kept my eye on where I wanted to go, and let him carry on going where he wanted to go.

This is a lesson we can learn from sports.

That's why boxers, footballers, even cricketers, insult each other during the match.

If your opponent can distract you, they can win.

If they can make you lose your temper, you stop thinking clearly.

You leave your rational mind, and go into your emotional mind.

And then you're not so good.

And then they win.

As Buddha said, "Act, don't react." ■

IF YOU DON'T DO IT, IT WON'T HAPPEN

My big sister was always the tough guy in our family.

I was always sitting around reading comics while she was out winning medals, and cups, and prizes.

So she was my role model for how powerful women were.

London was too slow, too old fashioned and lazy for her.

So, when I was 15, she went to live and work in New York.

When I was 18 I decided to go to art school.

But I got turned down by 7 art schools, from all over the UK.

I wrote to my sister and told her.

She said, "Screw them, come to art school in New York."

I wrote back, that was all very well, but we could never afford it.

She said, "Don't worry about it, we'll get you a scholarship."

I didn't expect anything to come of it, but next day the phone rang at home.

It was my sister calling from New York.

She said, "I'm sending you the application forms, you need to fill them in immediately, because they have to be in by the day after tomorrow."

I told her that wasn't possible.

It takes 4 days for airmail to get to the UK, and 4 days to get back again.

She said, "I know that. Just be at Heathrow airport tomorrow morning at 10am and ask for the captain on TWA flight 107."
And she hung up.

So the next morning I went to Heathrow.

He was waiting for me, at the TWA counter, with a bunch of forms in his hand.

He'd just flown a Boeing 707 in from New York.

He said, "Son, I have to wait here and make sure you fill these forms in. Then I have to take them back with me on tomorrow's return flight."

It turned out my sister had gone to JFK airport and located a flight that was going to London.

Then she chatted up the captain into bringing the forms over for me.

And then bringing them back again.

I thanked him as I filled the forms in.

He said, "Son, your sister is a very powerful lady."

And of course he was right.

Which is why my sister went to New York.

There, when you had a really great, outrageous, exciting idea, all the agreement was to help you make it happen.

It was a 'can do' culture.

I was used to the English way: great ideas that never happen.

I knew I had no chance of going to art school in New York.

Nice dream, but everyone agreed it was impossible.

I was resigned to accepting reality in London.

In which case I'd never have gone to art school.

And never have gone into advertising.

It would have stayed a nice dream.

The difference was my sister. She made it happen.

And that's what I learned from her.

If no one makes it happen, it doesn't happen. ■

WE STOP US

A guy I know told me a story about when he was growing up.

He said his dad worked away from home a lot.

The family: mum, two sons, one daughter, lived together in
a largish house.

The father lived, Monday to Friday, in a flat a long way away.

He usually came home to visit the family at weekends.

Everyone knew the dad didn't have much time for the family.

They knew he preferred to work away from home.

They knew it because whenever he came home he was in
a bad mood.

He didn't say much to anyone.

So the atmosphere was quite frigid.

He was grumpy and couldn't wait to get away, back to his job.

So they knew he felt distant from the family.

At least that was their reality.

However, this guy had a reconciliation with his dad before he died.

He asked his dad why he didn't like coming home.

His dad said,

"Are you crazy?

I couldn't get a decent job near where we lived.

But I wanted my family to have the best life I could provide.

So I eventually found a better paying job, but it meant working
in a different town.

I didn't want to disrupt everyone, so I went on my own.

But I absolutely hated leaving my family.

All week I used to sit in my little flat on my own, and dream about the weekend and coming home.

How thrilled you'd all be to see me, how we'd all hug each other.

How you'd tell me all the things you'd been up to all week.

And you'd want to know what had happened to me.

But when I walked in the door, no one wanted to talk to me.

Everyone just looked up, and went back to watching TV.

I'd been away all week from the thing I wanted most.

I'd been doing nothing but working all day, and coming back to the flat on my own at night.

Just so my family could have a good life.

And no one cared.

No one was grateful and no one wanted to talk to me,

so I didn't talk."

No wonder he got upset.

His reality was that he was sacrificing everything for the good of his family.

But he never told his family this.

He expected them to know.

But the family didn't know, because he never told them.

Their reality was, he can't love us because he keeps leaving us.

And each thought theirs was the only reality.

It never crossed their minds that their reality was just an interpretation.

So they lived it and, by living it, reinforced the interpretation.

Until it eventually became the reality.

Even though it wasn't.

And if that guy hadn't talked to his dad about it, before he died, they'd never have known.

Think about that next time you think you know what someone else's reality is.

Like when you think you know what your creative director is thinking.

When you think he doesn't like you, for whatever reason.

Or when you think you know what everyone in advertising thinks about you.

When you think they all think you're too old.

Or they think you haven't won enough awards.

Or you're just not trendy enough.

Or you're too cocky.

Or when you let your interpretation of other people's realities stop you.

You worry they'll think you're too arrogant.

Or they'll think you're a suck-up.

Or they'll laugh at you.

When you let something that doesn't even exist control your life.

See we don't live in reality.

We live in our interpretation of reality.

And that's what stops us.

Us. ■

DIRTY HARRIET

My big sister works in New York.

She is in charge of fundraising for the Chemotherapy Foundation.

As you can imagine, getting money out of New Yorkers is a

tough job.

But she likes it: she like a challenge.

Which is why she likes New York.

She works 6 days a week, 12 hours a day.

One evening, after work, she went to the cashpoint

(not smart at 11pm).

She couldn't find a cab so she decided to take the subway uptown

(also not smart at 11pm).

At the top of the subway steps she felt something in her back.

A voice said, "Lady this is a gun. Give me the money and no one

has to get hurt."

She turned around, looked the guy in the eyes and said,

"Wrong. You do."

Then she grabbed his coat lapels, kneed him in the balls and fell

backwards, dragging him with her to the bottom of the subway

steps.

They were rolling around on the floor, punching and kicking.

Then, my sister said, "Dammit. A transit cop came up and hauled

me off him."

The guy was arrested and convicted.

My sister got a letter of commendation from the District Attorney.

I said to her, "That's all very well Shirl, but if you'd been killed I'm the one who would have to tell Mum and Dad."

She said, "What can I tell you Dave? I looked in his eyes and I knew I could take him."

That's why my sister loves New York.

It's a can-do town.

And it's no place for shy people.

Advertising is also no place for shy people.

They have an expression that sums up New York,

"The squeaky wheel gets the oil."

They think that's logical.

If a wheel squeaks it needs oil.

If it doesn't squeak, it doesn't need oil.

So, if you want something, you need to make a noise.

You need to let whoever has got it know that you want it.

You need to let them know why they should give it to you.

You need to actively do something.

Not just passively sit there and hope it happens.

That's how advertising works.

And that's why good advertising started in New York. ■

A WIFE IS A DIFFERENT BRIEF

Years back at BMP I was interviewing an art director.

It started badly.

She pulled six ads out of her book for Stanley tools.

They were beautifully shot by David Thorpe, high contrast, the tools looked great.

I said, "That's one ad, where's the rest."

She said, "That's not one ad, that's six ads."

I said, "It's six photographs, but they've all got the same headline on: so that's one ad."

She said, "Don't be ridiculous, how can that be one ad?"

I said, "The same headline done six times doesn't make it six different ads."

The interview started badly and went downhill from there.

I said, "What are you earning?"

She told me.

I said, "Well we can only pay half of that."

She said, "Half, why?"

I said, "Well, for an art director that does the same headline on six different photographs."

She walked out, and that was that.

Except about six months later John Webster saw some of her work and asked her to come in for an interview.

But by now she already had a job, working for David Abbott.

So she said, "No thank you. I don't want to work at BMP if everyone's as rude as Dave Trott."

So that was that.

Except we met again, socially, about a year later.

Outside work we got on really well.

In fact we've been married thirty years now.

How does that work?

Inside work: a huge argument, outside work: a lifetime relationship?

The answer is, it's a different brief.

For me, the requirements for an art director are different to the requirements for a wife.

The brief for an art director is someone who's going to help me do better ads.

That's it.

We don't have to hold hands, or be friends, we don't have to socialise, we don't even have to like each other.

None of those things are wrong, they're just not the brief.

The brief isn't about looking for someone you like.

The brief is all about the work.

But when I'm looking for a life partner, that's not the brief at all.

In fact it's the exact opposite.

Here the brief is all about everything that the other brief wasn't about.

Someone who's going to make me happy, someone who I do want to spend all my time outside work with.

Someone I find attractive and exciting.

Totally different brief.

And that's the way it is in real life.

All the time we have totally different briefs that require totally different solutions.

And yet, in advertising, we think every single problem can only ever have one type of brief.

That's why every agency has one type of briefing form.

And every problem gets shoe-horned into that template.

And every answer looks the same.

As they say, "When the only tool you've got is a hammer, every problem starts to look like a nail." ■

NO ONE KNOWS WHAT'S IN YOUR HEAD

One of the first campaigns I ever did was for Pepsi.

"LIPSMACKINTHIRSTQUENCHINACETASTINGMOTIVATINGO
ODBUZZINCOOLTALKINHIGHWALKINGFASTLIVINEVERGIVI
NCOOLFIZZIN....."

The first commercial featured a guy trying to chat up a girl who only speaks Swedish.

As he realises he's wasting his time, he turns to camera and raises his eyebrows.

I thought this should have been quite subtle.

But, as I was only a junior, I wasn't invited to be involved with any of the production.

John Webster was not only the creative director, he was also directing the commercials.

So he did all the pre-production, casting, and shooting on his own.

When I saw it, we had a huge row.

Although I was a junior I was upset that everyone, even the account men, had seen the finished commercials before I had.

Probably this put me in a bad mood and made me dislike what he'd shot.

I thought everything was embarrassingly over the top.

The casting, the reaction shots, the acting.

None of it matched what was in my head.

So I refused to have it on my reel.

Until gradually the campaign began to take off.

It turned out John was right, the broad humour worked.

People saw it and laughed, simple as that.

I was the only person judging it against the version that was in my head.

The campaign became massively successful and I quietly put it back on my reel.

A year or so later there was a problem with the Mazola account.

The brief was about the higher temperatures that corn oil cooked at.

These higher temperatures sealed in the flavour of food.

Jane Newman, who was the planner on the account, said we needed a mnemonic.

No one else could come up with one, so to solve a problem I did.

Every vegetable would have its own safe.

Big safes for potatoes, lots of little safes for peas, long thin safes for chips, you get the idea.

I was a bit embarrassed about it, so I didn't put it on my reel.

Until sales of Mazola began to take off.

And CEOs of ad agencies began trying to find out who came up with the idea.

It was written up in Campaign as a professional solution,

"Not so much a creative's idea as a creative director's idea."

They didn't care that it wouldn't win any awards.

They were impressed at how quickly it put Mazola firmly on the map.

They weren't comparing it against what was in my head.

I quietly put the campaign back on my reel.

I find this a lot.

If the final film is the same as what's in our heads, we accept that because we're comfortable with it.

It's expected.

But if it's not what's in our head, we're disappointed.

We feel let down.

That's why it's worth remembering, we could be wrong.

We have to keep an open mind.

When anyone's putting a book or reel together, it's worth remembering that what we have in our head isn't the be-all and end-all of possibilities.

Because we're the only ones who know what's in our head.

And maybe we're blowing it out of proportion.

Maybe the difference only exists in our heads.

We're looking at everything under a jeweller's eyepiece.

To us differences from our original vision are magnified enormously.

But we have to forget what's in our head.

We have to be able to stand back and judge it as if we'd never even heard the idea before.

And that's hard to do.

And that's another thing I learned from John Webster. ■

NO RISK, NO REWARD

Before I went to art school in New York I needed to get a visa.

At the same time, a guy I knew wanted to travel to Chicago to visit the blues clubs.

So he came to the American embassy with me to get his visa.

We filled in the forms together, and then we were called in for an interview.

Afterwards we met up.

I said I'd got my visa and asked how he got on.

He said, "I can't believe it, they turned me down."

I asked, how come?

He said, "You know the questions where it says, 'Have you ever used drugs? If so explain'?"

I said yes.

He said, "Well I answered that I had used marijuana, mainly for listening to music. I was honest, and they didn't give me visa."

I said, "No shit."

So I went to America and he didn't.

See, I don't think my mate lost his visa for taking drugs.

I think he lost it for being stupid.

Did he really think that if he admitted taking drugs they'd admire his honesty and give him a visa?

Wake up.

When I left art school in New York I decided I wanted to work on a tramp steamer.

I couldn't get on an American or British ship because the unions were too strong.

So I went to Brooklyn to try the Scandinavian shipping lines.

They had much looser regulations.

They only asked me three questions.

Had I ever worked on a ship before?

Did I have good eyesight?

Could I swim?

I told them I'd worked on coasters, mainly around Britain.

Of course I had perfect eyesight.

And I could swim a mile in light clothing.

Now that wasn't strictly true.

I'd never been on a boat in my life.

Without my contact lenses I was blind as a bat.

And I couldn't swim a stroke.

But I figured if I told them that they probably wouldn't give me the job.

And I really wanted to work on a tramp steamer going to South America.

So, to help them give me the job, I told them what they needed to hear.

It wasn't really a sensible thing to do.

One night in the Gulf of Mexico, I was on watch, on the bridge.

The ocean is pitch black at night.

The only people awake on the ship were me and the first mate.

He had binoculars and always saw things well before me.

So one particular night, when I thought I saw a light, I didn't even bother telling him.

After about half hour the light started to get bigger and bigger.

I thought I'd better double-check.

When I went to ask him, he was fast asleep and drunk.

I woke him up and straight away he ran over to the wheel and started to turn the ship.

The trouble was, the other light was another ship.

And they started to turn at the same time we did.

Towards us.

Everything happens in slow motion at sea.

The first mate started to turn our ship away from them.

Again, just at the same time as they turned in the same direction.

Our two ships were zig-zagging towards each other across the Gulf of Mexico.

Eventually the other ship just barely missed us.

It passed so closely, and was so brightly lit, that we could see absolutely every rivet.

It was an American aircraft carrier.

Roughly ten times our size.

With hundreds of sailors lining the deck screaming at us.

Anyway, a few months later, when we got back to New York,

I wanted to get off the ship.

The captain was drunk and wouldn't sign me off.

So I jumped ship.

Because I'd been at art school in New York for four years,

I'd forgotten it wasn't my country.

Which meant I was now an illegal immigrant.

About a month later I was living in a flat in Manhattan when the door buzzer went.

I looked through the spyhole and it was a guy in a trench coat.

He kept buzzing the doorbell so I went out the fire escape.

One of the neighbours must have reported me, because when I got to the roof he was already there, with his gun out.

He took me downtown to The Battery, and locked me up in a cage, with lots of other illegal immigrants.

They were going to send me back to the ship in handcuffs.

Even though the ship was now up around Canada.

But I got lucky.

One guy checked my visa and decided I was still technically a student.

And, as a post grad, my visa allowed me to stay in America for a year.

But only if I was working.

So I had to go to Madison Avenue and get a job.

And actually I got lucky and it all worked out okay.

My point is, that was a pretty stupid risk I took, but I learned from it.

I learned never take a risk that can kill you.

But I also learned: no risk, no reward.

And, by and large, no risk that you take in advertising can kill you. ■

KNOW WHERE YOUR PARACHUTE IS

I'm a nervous guy. I don't like flying.

So the first thing I do when I sit down on a plane is take out the card from the back of the seat in front of me.

The one with all the emergency exit locations on.

Then I look all around and memorise where they are.

I memorise how they open.

Some exits, called A, open by moving the handle clockwise.

Some exits, called B, open by pulling the handle towards you.

I memorise how many rows of seats are between me and the nearest exit.

I figure, when the plane is on fire, it won't be the best time to wish I'd checked out these details.

When I've done all this I can relax a bit, because I've done as much as I can.

Is it a waste of time?

Maybe.

But I subscribe to Pascal's Wager.

Pascal's position was that it made more sense to believe in God than not to.

If there was a God, by worshipping it you'd have a wonderful after-life.

And be better off than the atheists, who would be burning in hell.

If there wasn't a God, well you'd be in the same boat as the atheists.

No after-life for anyone.

So on balance, it's a 50% better bet to believe in God than not to believe.

I feel like that about flying.

What I do is insurance.

If the plane reaches its destination safely, I've wasted 10 minutes studying the exits.

If we crash on the way, I have an advantage.

And I just may be in a better position to survive.

So, when the guy next to me is sipping his champagne, wondering why is that nut studying exits, I'm using the time he's wasting.

This need to go further than other people works for me.

When I was at BMP, John Webster said I could hire a young team to work under me.

In those days people didn't go around in teams, so I asked the head-hunter to find me a good young art director and writer I could put together.

I looked at lots of young art directors' books, but none of them were great.

Then the head-hunter told me there was a very good young art director at an agency called Vernons.

I asked her if she'd get him to send his book in.

She called back and said he didn't want to send his book in.

He was very junior and a bit shy, and didn't think he was ready for BMP.

I had a friend at Vernons, so I called them and asked about this kid.

They said, yes, he was good.

So that night after work I went over to Vernons to see my friend for a drink.

While I was there I asked them where the young art director sat.

They showed me his office.

Everyone had gone home, so I went in and looked around.

I found his portfolio and went through it, and it was good.

So the next day I called him up and said, "You don't have to come in for an interview, but I've seen your book and I'll give you the job."

That young, shy art director was Gordon Smith.

We've worked together for many years since then.

We've opened three different agencies, and won lots of awards.

All because, when the head hunter said no, I didn't let it stop there.

It would have been very easy to think, "Well she's the expert.

If she says he doesn't want to come I'd better leave it there."

That would have been the sensible thing to think.

Like thinking, "What's the point in worrying about the exits?

If the plane crashes, we're all dead anyway."

Well of course you can think like that.

Those are very good reasons for not doing anything.

There are always good reasons for not doing anything.

But by accepting those reasons, you've just thrown away whatever advantage you could have had. ■

NOTHING IS WRONG, JUST INAPPROPRIATE

When my children were between six and eight years old they discovered swearing.

They thought it was very daring and funny.

And, while it was just "Bum, Poo, Willy" I did too.

But then it graduated into serious swearing, and I had to think about how to approach it.

For a start, I'd need to be consistent.

I need to behave, myself, the way I'm telling my children to behave.

So, just like doing an ad, let's go back and research the brief.

What's wrong with swearing in the first place?

When do I do it, when don't I do it?

And why?

If I understand that I've got a brief from which to communicate.

So I got the kids to sit on the couch with me.

I said I wanted to have a chat about swearing.

And I said, "Here's what I know: Fuck, Cunt, Shit, Piss, Arsehole, Bastard, Turd, Prick."

Then I thought for a minute, just to check I hadn't missed any out.

And I said, "Yup, that's about it: Fuck, Cunt, Shit, Piss, Arsehole, Bastard, Turd, Prick."

The children were sitting there open-mouthed.

I said,

"Now they're just words.

There's absolutely nothing wrong with them at all, they're just words.

But what is wrong is bad manners.

What is wrong is making other people feel uncomfortable or bad, right?"

The children agreed, they were good kids.

They didn't want to hurt anyone's feelings.

I said, "Okay, so some people will be hurt and embarrassed if you use those words in front of them, and some people won't.

What we have to do is learn which is which."

They both nodded.

I said, "So it's fine if you want to use those words in front of me or my mates, we don't mind.

But we'd never use them in front of your mum, or your grandmas, or your teachers, or anyone who would be embarrassed, right?"

They both nodded because it made sense.

I said, "So here's the deal, before you swear you need to check that the other person doesn't mind. If they say they don't, then go ahead.

But if you think they might not like it, then don't do it."

A week or so later my kids came into the agency.

I was in one of the glass rooms talking to some of the guys.

My children came in, and my son said,

"Do you mind if I swear?"

The guys looked at me and said, "Er, no, not really."

My daughter said,

"Well I do. So I'll wait outside while you do it."

So she went outside and shut the door and watched through the glass.

My son stood inside and swore a bit.

Then she opened the door and said,

"Have you finished?" and came in.

Now that she knew she could swear, she no longer felt she had to swear.

Instead of just fighting against a set of rules, she understood how it worked.

Which meant she had control.

And not-swearing felt as empowering as swearing.

So how does that translate for us?

Well, we're in the communication business.

My feelings about conversations with children are the same as my feelings about all the forms of communication we do.

If it's the right thing to do we must be able to explain it.

If we can't explain it maybe it isn't the right thing to do. ■

PEOPLE DON'T THINK LIKE WE THINK THEY SHOULD THINK

Every time there was an election, exactly the same thing happened in our house.

Dad would come home from work, Mum would put his tea (dinner nowadays) in the oven to stay warm.

Then they'd go to the polls together.

Mum would vote Labour, Dad would vote Conservative.

Then they'd come home and Mum would get Dad's tea up.

There were no big political confrontations.

They were just exercising their right, and fulfilling their obligation, to vote.

I was always told, "People fought a war for our right to vote."

So what mattered was that they voted, not how they voted.

That was their right.

That was just a healthy difference of opinion.

Mind you, this was in the days before media pundits decided differing political views were fundamentally incompatible.

In the world before planners and marketing departments.

Nowadays that would be a household made up of two representatives of opposite, mutually incompatible, hostile psychographic groups.

But Mum and Dad, being ordinary people, didn't know they were supposed to behave like that.

So they didn't.

Them and millions of others.

They voted and that was that.

That's what people do, that's how they live their lives.

They don't do things according to the tramlines media gurus lay down.

They don't stay within the boxes we've got them in.

They don't think and act the way we think they should.

That's what free will is.

I was discussing this with Ken Livingstone once.

We'd just finished doing an anti Third World Debt commercial.

We were talking about Margaret Thatcher as the only politician that understood the working class.

Ken agreed, being working class himself he knew what I meant.

The Labour party had become the party of the Left.

That's not the same as the working class.

I told him that my mum had voted Labour ever since she'd been old enough to vote, in the 1920s.

Then in 1984, after my dad died, she went to vote on her own.

I said to her, "I suppose you voted Labour as usual?"

She said, "No, I voted Conservative."

I was gobsmacked after over 50 years of voting Labour.

I asked Mum why she'd done that.

She said, "Did you see that old man on TV on Remembrance Sunday at the Cenotaph, wearing a donkey jacket? At least Mrs Thatcher showed the proper respect and dressed smartly."

Ken Livingstone sat there shaking his head, saying, "I know, I know, poor Michael never understood the working class. He thought he was showing solidarity with them."

People don't do what they're supposed to do.

The working class don't do what The Guardian thinks they should do.

They vote with their hearts not their heads.

Because that's what we all do.

When we media professionals strategise about advertising, it's rational and logical, as if all people will behave according to our plans.

Then, when we leave the office, we become consumers and do exactly what our emotions tell us we should do.

That's why it's our job to excite people, not to try to herd them.

We have to make a case in the simplest, most memorable, way we can.

Then get out of the way.

There's security in hiding behind long words and convoluted thinking, but no real power.

We have to go beyond the complicated to get to the simple.

Over 2,000 years ago, Democritus said,

"The mind is not a vessel to be filled, but a fire to be ignited."

People, all of us, are simpler than we want to believe.

Advertising, all of it, is simpler than we want it to be.

I'm convinced, in communication, simplicity is power.

But three of my heroes: Brian Clough, Bill Bernbach, and Ron Greenwood, all felt even more strongly.

They all said, "Simplicity is genius." ■

WHAT MADE MIKE MYERS BETTER?

Mike Myers took Hollywood by storm.

They didn't see him coming.

His brand of humour was so quirky, so odd.

I read an interview with him about this.

They asked him what were the influences that made him so different to mainstream American humour.

He said it was partly because he was a Canadian.

His mum and dad had emigrated from Liverpool.

They knew they were going to miss home.

So they brought the things they thought they'd really miss most of all.

Tapes of their favourite radio programmes.

'The Goon Show', 'Around The Horn', 'Hancock's Half Hour'.

Things you can't get anywhere else.

See, in America, TV pretty much killed traditional radio.

Now it's mainly just background, something you have on while you're doing something else.

Driving, housework, hobbies.

So it has to be about things you don't need to concentrate on.

Music and phone-ins.

Whereas BBC radio still assumes people will actually sit down and listen.

So you have comedy programmes, quiz shows, radio plays, long-running serials.

Pretty much like TV, but without the pictures.

Which meant it was faster and cheaper to make than TV.

Which meant it could be more experimental.

Mike Myers grew up listening to his parents' tapes.

Which gave him a whole dimension of humour that America didn't have.

They'd just been brought up on TV.

I've always thought the limitations of radio are what made it great.

Because it doesn't have pictures, it develops your imagination muscle.

That's great for children.

When my kids were young it was always difficult to get them to bed.

So I thought, let's take that as a brief.

First let's investigate the problem.

Children want entertainment but, like everyone else, they're basically lazy.

They want to just sit up and watch TV, and let it do all the work.

But maybe there's compromise here that works for both of us.

They'd like entertainment, but I'd like them to use their brain.

So I bought a lot of old-fashioned radio plays on tape.

At night I would put them to bed, switch the lights out, give them a torch, and let them listen in the dark.

I'd put on Sherlock Holmes or Raymond Chandler, or 'Orson Welles' Tales From The Black Museum'.

Radio plays are really melodramatic.

The SFX and music have to help tell the story and set the mood.

So they were atmospheric, and a little scary.

And mainly, what I liked, is the children had to use their imaginations.

While they were listening to the story, their minds were creating the pictures.

They were participants, not just recipients.

Developing their imaginations.

Spike Milligan worked better on the radio than TV.

Because he used sound effects in 'The Goons' to create images that are much funnier for being suggested rather than shown.

Tony Hancock worked better on radio than TV.

Because he used 'dead-air' to make what you imagine happening much funnier than if you saw it.

TV first became big in the USA, back in the 1950s and clients began shifting their ad budgets to it.

The radio companies asked comedian Stan Freberg to do a commercial telling clients why they should advertise on radio.

This is roughly what he did:

Announcer: "This is a live news broadcast and we're about to witness an incredible event.

Lake Michigan, the second largest lake in the entire world, has been filled with billions of gallons of whipped cream.

And now a giant B52 bomber is about to drop a 50 ton maraschino cherry right into the middle of it, from a height of 20,000 feet."

SFX: *Jet engine noise*

Announcer: "And here it comes, ladies and gentlemen, what an incredible sight, what an historic moment."

SFX: whistling noise

Announcer: "And there it goes ladies and gentlemen, right on target."

SFX: whistling noise

Announcer: " And it's about to hit, it's about to hit, THERE IT GOES."

SFX: splodge!!!

Announcer: "Well there you have it ladies and gentlemen: a 50 ton maraschino cherry dropped from a B52 bomber into Lake Michigan filled with whipped cream.

Let's see you do that on TV." ■

SOUND IS MORE POWERFUL THAN VISION

Most of us who make commercials believe that the visuals are the most important part.

This is because the visuals are the most obvious part.

Which, of course, is why visuals are what win awards.

Which, in turn, is why we care more about visuals.

And so on.

We act as if sound was merely there to decorate the pictures.

But actually, when we do this we're only operating in one dimension.

This happens because the sound is the part we don't notice.

But in the real world (the world outside awards juries) it often has a bigger effect than the part that we do notice.

When my children were small they'd sometimes watch scary movies on TV.

Sometimes they'd get really frightened.

Because I didn't want them to get nightmares, I'd just turn the sound off.

Then let them watch for a while with no sound.

So they could see what was scaring them was their imagination.

Which is where sound works.

You know what, horror movies aren't nearly so scary without sound.

Kubrick was one of the few directors who understood sound.

That's why he'd use it as a counter-point for the visual.

Not just to decorate it, but to amplify it.

Take Clockwork Orange.

The part where the thugs kick a tramp to death in the underpass.

Not just to the grunts and thumps you'd expect.

Or even a violent heavy-metal track.

But instead, they kick him to death to the lyrical melody 'Singing In The Rain'.

Because it's the opposite of the visual it makes it so much more powerful.

Like the marines at the end of Full Metal Jacket.

Marching away from death and destruction and a ruined city.

But not to the Rolling Stones singing, 'Paint it Black', as you'd expect.

They're all marching off singing The Mickey Mouse Club Theme Tune.

Trained killers joining together in an innocent children's song.

That was Eisenstein's theory of film: 1+1=3.

Sound can change what we're looking at.

The BBC showed the same footage twice, of the burning oil wells of Kuwait after the first Gulf war.

First they showed the footage with Chris Rea's 'Road To Hell'.

Then they showed it with Mozart's Requiem.

Totally different experience.

One track made the visuals graphic and exciting.

The other track made them a sad, timeless comment on mankind.

When I was at college in New York, there were two public broadcast channels.

One on radio (WBAI), the other on TV (Channel 13).

They were both viewer/listener sponsored, so there were no commercials.

Consequently they could be more experimental.

One time I remember they showed a two-hour film by an experimental animator called Fred Mogubgub.

They played one soundtrack on the TV against the picture, and a totally different soundtrack on the radio.

Then every 10 minutes they'd remind you to switch from one to the other, to see how it changed the pictures you were watching.

It was a great lesson in how sound can dictate vision.

How our imagination can dictate what we see.

Over here, Channel 5 did a similar thing a few years back with London Live 94.9 FM.

They showed a football game between (I think) Spurs and Liverpool.

Channel 5 broadcast the serious commentary to go with the game.

London Live 94.9 FM broadcast a commentary from two Australian comedians, watching the game live on a TV in the car park outside the stadium.

The commentary on the radio added way more to the game than the TV commentary, which was just decoration for the visuals.

They only did it the once but, if I could, I'd watch every game that way.

"How stupid does that goalie feel missing a sitter like that?"

"Yeah, and look at that haircut, what a wally."

"Hey mate, your whole family's watching and you just blew it."

It actually made watching it on TV a better experience than going to the game.

Finally, to prove how important sound is, find someone who's not in advertising.

Ask them what they remember about Hovis advertising.

I bet it won't be Ridley Scott's fantastic camera-work they talk about.

I bet they start to whistle or hum a snatch of Dvorak's New World Symphony, played by a colliery brass band.

And that ran 30 years ago.

It's not the visuals that the public take off the screen, and get passed into the language.

It's the sound.

Sound was viral long before YouTube. ■

OBJECTIVE - GOOD. SUBJECTIVE - BAD

I recently spent 4 days on a jury judging D&AD TV & Cinema.

There were about 1,500 ads from Shanghai, Taiwan, Bangkok, Israel, USA, South America, the Middle East, ex member-states of the old USSR, you name it.

There were 22 people on the jury, about half from the UK.

The others were from Paris, New York, Toronto, Buenos Aires, Australia, Colorado, you name it.

So it was a very interesting mix.

Ads from all around the world, judged by people from all around the world.

Truly international.

And I found that difficult.

Especially when we got to the discussion stage.

Because each member of the jury would begin talking about an ad by saying, "I like it."

Or they'd say, "I don't like."

Whether it was an American talking about a Chinese ad, or a German talking about a Brazilian ad, or a Canadian talking about a Russian ad.

"I like it."

"I don't like it."

I found that difficult because it's one of the first things I teach students not to do.

When we're simply a consumer, we react to advertising.

That's all we need to do, just react.

So we can be subjective: we don't have to think about it.

But when we become a professional we can't do that.

We can't carry on reacting without thinking.

Now we have to be in charge of how other people react.

We have to make them react in a certain way.

And to do that we have to be OBjective not SUBjective.

We have to remove ourselves and our personal tastes.

We're not simply experiencing a piece of advertising anymore.

Now we're doing a job.

Now we're professionals.

We have to think about what we're doing.

So we no longer say, "I like it", or "I don't like it".

Now we must always begin a criticism with, "It works because…".

Or, "It doesn't work because…".

Using this language forces us to fill in the second part of the sentence.

It forces us to back up our opinion.

It forces us to explain.

And that forces us to think.

And that forces us to behave like professionals.

Objectively, not subjectively.

That's why I always encourage students to train their minds by always using the correct language.

"I like it" is wrong on two counts.

Number one, it talks about, "I" and that's wrong.

We are not the target market, so we're not important.

Number two, it says "like it".

That's a feeling, not a thought.

So that expression has no place in an objective discussion about a piece of work.

On the other hand, "It works because…" is right on three counts.

Number one: "It", we're talking about the piece of work, not just someone's opinion.

Number two: "works", we're talking about the function it's supposed to deliver, not how it makes us feel.

Number three: "because", we have to back up what we say, with reasoned argument.

And it's very hard to have a rational debate with an emotional response, such as "I like it" or "I don't like it." ■

WHEN YOU TRAIN STUDENTS, YOU TRAIN YOURSELF

Over the years I've always had classes of students come into the agency in the evenings.

Sometimes it might be for just one or two sessions, sometimes for ten.

It depends how many of the creative department are interested in taking a class.

Each class consists of about 15-20 students.

You set them a brief the week before, then on the night they bring their work along for a crit.

I always encourage everyone in the creative department to teach at least one class.

I believe while our copywriters and art directors are training the students, they're being trained themselves.

To be creative directors.

You see each class is a crash course in running a creative department.

Writers and art directors have just a couple of hours to look at up to 20 campaigns.

In that time they have to work out what's right or wrong about the research, the strategy, the media choice, the creative idea, the copywriting, and the art direction of each campaign.

And they have to be able to explain what to do about it in a clear, simple way.

Great training in fast, powerful, clear thinking.

And, if the students question or argue it's a test of how good that thinking is.

So while they're teaching the students, the students are teaching them.

And everyone develops their own style of teaching.

Personally, I just give students the name of the product and nothing else.

They have to do their own brief, their own research, and their own media.

Before they start writing ads.

Then everyone in the class sticks all their ads on the walls together, so we can refer back and forth during the crit.

Gordon Smith doesn't do this, he's an art director so he's more considered.

He likes the campaigns presented one at a time.

But there's one terrific thing he does.

He doesn't let the person who did the work present it.

He picks a different person to present it.

This works well because it's the first time the presenter has seen the work.

And if the idea isn't clear the presenter gets confused.

Just as the public would.

The person who did the ads can see they didn't communicate.

They may have understood what they did, but no one else does.

This makes the point that you don't get to sell what's in your head.

The ad either works on the page or it doesn't.

Very clear demonstration.

Anna and Elaine are a team that don't do either of these ways.

They like to do a fast strategy session.

So they don't brief anyone to do any ads for their class.

During the day, Anna and Elaine fill a cardboard box with a dozen or so different things lying around their office.

A packet of crisps, a toy, cleaning product, trainers, pen, iPod, biscuits.

Then they go into the class and everyone takes one product.

Then the students go off to different offices.

They get half an hour to come up with a strategy and campaign thought for their product.

Then they bring them back and stick them on the wall alongside everyone else's.

Everyone can see who's done some exciting strategic thinking, and who hasn't.

This is great for teaching students that real creativity starts with the strategy.

Not just the pictures and words.

It's also great to teach them not just to rely on planners to write the brief.

And of course, every time Anna and Elaine crit someone's strategic thinking, they learn more about running a department themselves.

Everyone gets trained.

And that's what's in it for me.

Both in training students and encouraging my department to train students.

For me that's how I've progressed through the system.

First I learned to do it.

Then I learned how to teach other people to do it.

Now I'm learning how to teach other people, to teach other people to do it.

It's the same rule for life.

If you set the game up right, everybody wins. ■

WHERE DOES AN IDEA COME FROM?

A few years ago I went to see an exhibition of the very latest in art at the Tate Modern.

They obviously hadn't finished installing it, because the workmen had left their paints and rollers on trestle tables, all covered by a dust sheet.

Also they'd left crisp packets and empty drinks cans lying around.

One of the cleaners was worried that he would get in trouble for leaving the gallery in such a mess.

So he stacked the tables away in a cupboard and threw the rest of the rubbish out.

It turned out that what he'd thrown out had actually been one of the works of art in the exhibition.

It was a big story next day, across all the newspapers.

But the best part for me was that The Sun immediately made the cleaner their Arts Correspondent.

They admired his taste.

Here was a man who could tell rubbish from art.

The Sun paid him to go round and review all the work on show at the different art galleries in London.

What a great example of finding something funny in real life and turning it into opportunity.

The strange thing is we spend all our time looking so hard for ideas.

But great things are happening all around us, all the time, that could be turned into ideas.

The playwright Alan Bennett says he gets lots of his ideas just from overhearing people talking, and making notes.

Peter Kay says the same thing, "You couldn't make it up."

Real life is often funnier than fiction.

And, for some reason, mums are a great source of dialogue.

During the power blackouts of the 1970s, I once heard my mum on the phone to my Auntie Polly.

Mum said, "What I don't understand is, if no one's got any electricity how come the cars have all got their lights on?"

Then a few days later, Auntie Polly phoned Mum again.

She said, "You'd better do your hoovering quick because they've just said on the news the price of electricity is going up."

But it isn't just mums.

There was van driver at BMP called George.

He said to me once, "Here Dave, you like books don't you? Do you want to buy some?"

I said, "It depends George, what sort of books are they?"

He said, "Big uns."

Huh?

And then some things are so good, you really couldn't make them up.

One day Gordon Smith said to me, "What I don't understand is, if we're all evolved from monkeys, how come there's still monkeys around?"

Fair point.

Al Midgeley, an art director at BMP, once told me he was sitting in a pub in Yorkshire reading the paper.

Two undertakers walked in, in top hats, silk gloves, everything black.

They each got a pint and sat at the table next to him.

Then they drank their pints in absolute silence.

After about half an hour, one turned to the other and said,

"Death? It's a bugger."

Like Alan Bennett and Peter Kay, John Webster knew how to take ordinary things and turn them into ideas.

I was telling him once about a really old pub I used to drink in sometimes, in Barking.

It was called 'The Barge Aground' right near Barking Creek.

And it had a really old fashioned public bar with sawdust on the floor.

One old guy used to bring his dog in with him.

He'd order his pint, then ask the barman for an arrowroot biscuit and a saucer.

He'd make the dog lie on the floor and put the biscuit on its paw.

And when the man would say, "Go" the dog would flip the biscuit into its mouth, and eat it.

The man would then pour some of his pint into the saucer for the dog.

I told John about it.

I thought it was just a funny story.

John said, "That's fantastic, we can use that."

And he did, and he won a black pencil.

And that's maybe the biggest lesson I learned from John.

It's not who says it, it's who spots it. ■

THE CREATIVE MAP

One of the greatest pieces of visual communication is the London tube map.

I never really appreciated it until I was taught about it, at art school in New York.

Cities the world over copy the basic principles of this design.

New York, Tokyo, Paris, Berlin, Singapore.

And yet I grew up with it, so I never thought anything of it.

What's so good about it? It's just a map.

Well no actually, it isn't.

It's not a map.

The routes that the tube lines follow, bear little relationship to where they actually go.

The distances bear no resemblance to reality either.

Even the Thames isn't that shape in real life.

According to this 'map' every tube line is perfectly straight or smoothly curved. And every line goes either vertically, horizontally, or 45 degrees.

No variaton.

Now of course that isn't anything like the reality.

If you've ever seen a map of the actual tube lines, it's like a cross between a spider's web and a cracked windscreen.

But the man who designed this map wasn't a cartographer.

He wasn't even a graphic designer.

He was a draughtsman, called Harry Beck.

So he didn't do a map, or an attractive layout.

He did a wiring diagram.

If you've ever tried to trace the electrics on a car you'll know what I mean.

The diagram doesn't show you an accurate drawing of the route of the wire.

It shows you a start point at (say) the battery.

Then a straight line to the end point at (say) a bulb.

You don't need a map, you go to the car and trace the actual route yourself.

That's how the tube 'map' works.

You're underground, everything is identical: just a tunnel.

It doesn't matter what's going on above.

You need to know the start point, and the finish point.

In the simplest possible way.

What an absolutely stunningly brilliant piece of thinking.

The tube map isn't a map.

It's a wiring diagram.

Before he did it, it was a ridiculous thing to even suggest.

Since he did it, everyone in the world copied it.

Isn't that a great lesson for us?

People can't agree with a great thought before it's done.

Because, if it's a great thought, it breaks the rules.

And you can't agree that breaking the rules makes sense because it doesn't.

Following the rules makes sense.

That's why we have rules.

Breaking the rules won't work.

Until it does.

Then everyone can agree.

And, of course, it's the same in advertising.

Breaking the rules won't get any agreement.

If you ask for permission you won't get it.

But once you break the rules, and it works, people can see it makes sense.

Then that becomes part of the new rules.

Which can't be broken.

That's how it goes.

If you wait for permission, you'll never get into trouble.

You can't be wrong, but you can't do anything truly exciting either.

Helmut Krone was one of the greatest art directors ever.

He did two of the all-time best advertising campaigns.

He said,

"If you can look at something and say 'I like it' then it isn't new." ■

IS ADVERTISING A CON?

Advertising started with the snake-oil salesmen in the Wild West.
They didn't really have anything to sell except bottles of coloured water, which didn't actually do anything.

So all that was important was how these salesmen could charm the gullible public.

They admired and trusted the salesman, so they'd buy whatever he was selling.

As people gradually became more educated, this resulted in advertising getting a bad reputation.

Just like used-car salesmen.

Who would avoid talking about the product, but would seduce you with their patter.

In 1950s America there was a reaction against this.

Manufacturers didn't want patronising advertising that was greeted with suspicion by their customers, and made the company look bad.

So the USP was born.

The Unique Selling Proposition.

Avoid smarmy salesmanship.

Stick to the facts.

Find something different about your product and say it.

So everyone copied that for a while.

And advertising became really boring.

"Our washing powder gets your clothes X% cleaner."

"Our car gives you X% more miles per gallon."

"Our washing machine spins X% faster."

"Our dishwasher is X% quieter."

"Our TV set gives you X% more colour."

This was a corruption of a good idea.

Finding something unique about your product is a great start point.

Finding a reason why someone should actually part with cash for what you make rather than what your competitor makes.

This is common sense if you're in the business of selling anything to anyone.

The problem is lazy thinking.

Finding any difference, no matter how small or irrelevant, and stopping there.

USP stands for Unique Selling Proposition.

The two magic words here are 'unique' and 'selling'.

What you talk about has to be unique, not just a marginal improvement on what everyone else offers.

Plus, for it to be 'selling', it has to be something that people truly want.

Not just any old point of difference.

Unique on its own isn't enough.

But lazy thinking meant that, as soon as anyone found any benefit, no matter how tiny, they called it a USP and did an ad.

Then the ads became all about delivering this information.

So the ads were dull, factual, purely informative.

And the USP got a bad name because of it.

It was replaced by the ESP.

The Emotional Selling Proposition.

This is the belief that, since information was boring, you don't have to say anything at all.

All that's important is how you say it.

So you have the latest fashion.

The rise of pure brand advertising.

All that matters is the brand, the product is unimportant.

Everyone is trying to say nothing in a very charming and seductive way.

A sort of postmodern Arthur Daley.

I've just finished reading a speech by Bill Bernbach.

He talks about the need for both emotion and reason.

Start with a fact, but don't stop there.

How you say something may well be more important than what you say.

But you have to have something to say in the first place.

If you have nothing to say that will soon be apparent.

No one will be fooled.

Think of it as an oyster.

You start with a piece of grit, and build a pearl around it.

People buy the pearl, they don't buy the grit.

But no grit, no pearl.

When you talk to someone about something you passionately believe in, they won't just buy the logic of your argument.

They'll also buy the passion with which you deliver it.

But if it's passion about nothing, they won't buy that either.

Because that's just back to snake-oil salesmen. ■

HITLER'S SOCKS

Years ago we used to do animatics, to test commercials
before they ran.

The best illustrator for this was a guy called Harry.

Harry had a rep called Al Spartley.

Al was from Essex, and drove a BMW.

One day Al told me he'd bought Hitler's socks.

My first question was, how much for?

Al said he'd paid £4,000 (and this is 20 years ago).

My second question was, why?

Who wants Hitler's socks?

Are they clean or dirty?

Are they worth more if they're washed in soap powder
or left soiled?

Can you smell Hitler's feet?

Al said it was a one-off chance to get Hitler's socks, and he
couldn't pass it up.

My next question was, how do you know they're Hitler's socks?

Have they got a little swastika pattern on them?

Al said he had a letter of authentication.

I repeated the question, how do you know they're Hitler's socks?

Hitler hasn't signed the socks has he?

They haven't got a serial number on.

How do you know someone didn't keep the letter, but switch
the socks?

Anyway, what does the letter say, "I, Adolf Hitler, hereby vouch for the authenticity of the attached footwear, and verify these are the socks worn by me during the establishment of the Third Reich."?

I found the whole thing very strange.

But that's what museums are based on I guess.

People are fascinated by things that they wouldn't otherwise notice.

Like a pair of socks.

Just because they belonged to someone famous.

So it's not the actual object itself that we like.

In fact it's everything that isn't the actual object that intrigues us.

It's what goes on in our heads about it.

I used to argue a lot with Paul Arden about Duchamp's bottle rack.

Why should I pay hundreds of thousands of pounds for that particular bottle rack, which isn't even signed?

If I think it's beautiful, why don't I pop down to the shops and buy the identical thing for around a tenner?

Paul said it isn't the same, that particular bottle rack is worth more because Marcel Duchamp chose it.

Like a photographer choosing an image with a camera, the artist chose that particular bottle rack.

Anything else is at best a copy.

While that may be intellectually true, even Duchamp couldn't tell the difference between that and another bottle rack.

And, personally, I think that was Duchamp's whole point.

It's a modern take on 'Beauty is in the eye of the beholder'.

I think he was saying the exact same things exist all around us and we don't even see them.

But put something in an art gallery and we notice it.

Because someone has told us that it has meaning.

That it ought to be separated off from everything else and considered as more worthy of our attention.

We don't trust ourselves to work out what things are valuable or not.

We let someone else, an expert, an artist, a museum curator, do that for us.

The same is true of awards.

We don't have the confidence to trust our own judgement about what's good and bad.

We need someone to do that for us.

Some certificate of verification that something is more worthy.

We need someone to tell us what's good.

That's why we are all so impressed by whoever has won more awards.

Because if they've won more awards it must mean they're better.

I think it's a bit like saying Michelangelo is a better artist than da Vinci because his paintings have more colours.

Van Gogh is a better painter than Gauguin because his work is in more museums.

Why do we need someone else's opinion to tell us what's worthwhile?

That's just like the 'Hitler's Socks' of the art world. ■

THERE'S A LOT OF ENERGY IN BEING NAUGHTY

When we got the Toshiba account, we found the main reason
people weren't buying them was the name.
To English ears, all the Japanese/Korean brands sounded the same.
A sort of mish-mash of oriental sounds,
'Aka-wara-tora-ichi-uji-itsibushi'.
So how could we separate Toshiba off from the rest?
How could we get it into the language?
Well 'Tosh' was a friendly expression that grownups used when
they ruffled the hair of children.
So we put that together with Alexei Sayle's song
'Hello John Gotta New Motor' and changed it to 'Hello Tosh
Gotta Toshiba'.
But research said Alexei's voice was too shrill.
We needed something softer and warmer to contrast the visual
of a robotic blueprint man.
I'd never met Ian Dury, but I really liked his voice.
He sounded like a big friendly cockney bear.
He agreed to do it and we met for the first time at the
recording studio.
Ian hadn't done any adverts before, and he was a bit suspicious
of advertising types.
He thought they were all flash toffs who drove Ferraris, wore
Rolexes, and used long words to blag gullible people.
But when we got talking he gradually loosened up a bit.

First he found out I was from Barking, not far from Upminster where he was from.

He said Barking was a rough area because he remembered reading about a Teddy Boy who'd been stabbed to death there in a fight, when he was a boy.

I said yes, that was my mate's big brother.

He was inside, doing 25 years for it.

So when Ian could see I wasn't a flash toff, he relaxed a bit.

Then, when Ian found out I'd been to art school like him, he relaxed even more.

He said he'd done his foundation year at West Ham Tech.

I'd done foundation, again not far away, at East Ham Tech.

On Ian's foundation course with him was Viv Stanshall, who later formed The Bonzo Dog Doo Dah Band.

A lot of people from that course ended up at The Royal College.

One of Ian's most influential teachers was Peter Blake, one of the founders of Pop Art.

But Peter Blake is probably more famous for doing the cover of The Beatles' 'Sergeant Pepper' album.

I always thought, if you look at Peter Blake's art and listen to Ian Dury's, or Viv Stanshall's songs, you can see the similarity in what they're doing.

They're using different mediums but the style and content is the same.

But then I think that's true of art and music generally.

Rococo, Neo-Classicism, Romanticism, are all parallel art and music movements.

Right up to Modern Art and Modern Jazz.

And even Abstract Expressionism and Free Form Jazz.

Anyway, we got on so well I asked Ian if he wanted to pop over to the house at Christmas for a drink.

Big mistake.

On Boxing Day, Ian tipped up absolutely rat-arsed.

He sat in the front room and started rolling a joint.

Normally this wouldn't have been a problem, but I had my family staying with me for Christmas.

So, sitting in the front room, was my mum (think of Irene Handel), my Uncle Harry (think Alf Garnett), my big sister Shirley, and my brother-in-law Jerry, both from New York.

Plus my wife Cathy, and my kids Jade and Lee.

None of these are used to your standard rock-star behaviour.

So I said, "Look Ian, it'll be much easier to roll a joint on the kitchen table."

And I quickly ushered him out of the front room and into the kitchen.

While he sat there in the kitchen struggling to put a spliff together the front doorbell rang.

I answered it and it was Peter Cook and his new wife.

Peter is famous as the father of modern satirical comedy, and was a bit of a wild man himself when he was younger.

But on this occasion Peter had just come back from his honeymoon.

He and his new wife were feeling very happy and loved-up.

So everyone was on their best behaviour.

I tried to get them into the front room to meet the family.

But a deep cockney voice yelled out, "OI. COOKIE."

Peter and his wife looked into the kitchen.

In a variety of accents Ian started shouting, "Peter fucking Cook....... Peter fucking Cook....... Peter fucking Cook....... Peter fucking Cook....... Peter fucking Cook....... Peter fucking Cook....... Peter fucking Cook....... Peter fucking Cook....... Peter fucking Cook....... Peter fucking Cook....... Peter fucking Cook....... Peter fucking Cook....... Peter fucking Cook....... Peter fucking Cook....... Peter fucking Cook....... "

(Those of you that have heard the 'Derek and Clive' album will get the reference.)

This went on for about 10 minutes and, inside Ian's head, it was the funniest thing he'd ever heard.

The trouble was everybody else, especially my family, wasn't inside Ian's head.

And they'd never heard 'Derek and Clive', so they didn't get the amusing reference.

After a massively frosty reception, Ian decided this wasn't going to be a rock and roll party after all, and I managed to bundle him into a cab.

I said to Peter Cook, "I'm sorry Peter, I've never seen Ian that pissed before."

Peter said, "I've never seen anyone that pissed before."

But I always liked Ian's outrageous behaviour.

I loved the way he always wanted to get into trouble.

To find out what he wasn't allowed to do, and do it.

Ian had polio when he was young.

This left him crippled for life, with a partially withered
arm and leg.

Two ways you can go in this situation.

You either let your life be about feeling sorry for yourself, and
why did it have to happen to you, it's so unfair.

Or you get in everyone's face about it and start taking the piss.

Ian chose the latter.

He always referred to himself as 'a raspberry'.

This is cockney rhyming slang for 'raspberry ripple' or cripple.

This is what you learn growing up in a tough environment.

To take the piss out of yourself first, and better than anyone else can.

That way you win because you're faster and funnier.

Which is why Ian wrote the song 'Spasticus Autisticus' all about
spastics (or 'raspberries').

The term 'spastic' had become a pejorative, and was even
shortened to 'spazz' as in "Don't be a spazz."

Ian decided to go exactly the other way and celebrate it with an
anthem that would catch on with everyone.

Of course the BBC banned it.

Which was exactly what he wanted.

To stick two fingers up to the establishment meant that a
'raspberry' could be as outrageous and rebellious as anyone.

With one song he almost made disability cool.

I liked Ian's attitude so much we even used one of his songs on the
agency answer-phone.

You know when you phone a company and the switchboard
operator puts you on hold.

You normally get a bland repetitive piece of music, like Pachelbel's Canon.

We put Ian Dury's 'Fucking Ada' on ours.

When the operator put you on hold, you'd hear a heavenly choir singing over and over again….

"Fucking Ada……..Fucking Ada…….Fucking Ada…….Fucking Ada………Fucking Ada…….Fucking Ada…..…..Fucking Ada…… Fucking Ada….Fucking Ada….Fucking Ada…….Fucking Ada…… Fucking Ada…. Fucking Ada…….Fucking Ada…….Fucking Ada…… …Fucking Ad………Fucking Ada…….Fucking Ada……."

Which, I reckon, is pretty much what everyone feels like when they're put on hold. ■

WE NEED SOME GUYS FROM BROOKLYN

I was talking to an American the other day.

He was a big, loud, funny guy and he had on a nice suit.

He was Jewish, and he was from Brooklyn.

He was in the oil import/export trade, and I asked him how
business was.

He said,

"It's really interesting: these WASPY guys from the CIA came to
see me."

I asked him what they wanted.

He said,

"These super-straight, buttoned-down guys came to my house.
They said they'd noticed that I did a lot of travelling to
the Middle East. They wanted to know if I'd gather intelligence
for them."

I said, "What did you say?"

He said,

"What do you think, I'm crazy? I told them I wouldn't actively go
out of my way, but if I saw anything I thought they could use, I'd let
them know about it."

I said, "What did they say to that?"

He said,

"They asked what sort of thing I thought I could spot that might
be useful."

I said, "What did you tell them?"

He said,

"Usually when the main fuel dump is half full they call up one of my tankers to come in and top it up. Supposing the fuel dump is completely empty, and they want the tankers to come and refill it? That could be because they've just filled up all their military vehicles ready for an invasion. I said I could tip them off about that?"

I said, "What did they say?"

He said,

"They were very impressed. They said that was really clever thinking and where exactly were these oil dumps? And that's when I realised, the CIA is never going to be any good until we get some guys from Brooklyn running it."

I feel the same way about advertising.

Everybody's studying marketing, reading the case histories, learning the rules.

Everyone's heads are full of what they are and aren't allowed to do.

So everyone is doing pretty much the same as everyone else.

One of the things you learn in Brooklyn is not to do that.

Not to play by the rules.

In the poorest part of a big city the rules are: the toughest guy wins.

So if you're not the toughest guy how can you win?

You learn to use your brain instead of your fists.

You learn to out-think people. You learn to turn things to your advantage.

And that's exactly what we should do in advertising.

How can we out-think the competition?

How can we turn what looks like a problem into an advantage?

An unfair advantage. Because all advantage is unfair.

Otherwise it wouldn't be an advantage.

I was walking through Hampstead this morning on the way to work.

A father was helping his son into school with his sports kit.

"May the best team win," he said as he waved goodbye.

I thought, you wouldn't hear that in Brooklyn. ■

ANDY MCNAB AND ADVERTISING

I was talking to a class of about 30 students from Newcastle the other night.

They were very quiet, as most students are nowadays.

They were waiting for me to tell them the right way to do advertising.

They'd probably seen half a dozen other creative directors on their trip down to London.

I'm sure everyone had given them their version of the right way to do advertising.

The students thought all they had to do was listen.

So they sat there listening.

No one said a word.

Everyone was too bored or frightened to speak.

And it was dull.

Dull for them.

Dull for me.

I tried to make the point that learning isn't passive, it's active.

You can't learn just by listening to someone else.

Mark McCormack, the sports agent, wrote a book about his profession: 'What They Don't Teach You At Harvard Business School'.

Someone said to him, "Yeah, but you're not going to give away any of your real secrets in your book are you?"

McCormack said, "Put it this way. Jack Nicklaus could tell you everything he's ever learned about golf. Then he could still take you on any golf course and whip your ass."

Making the point that you don't get great just by listening to other people.

So having another dull class wouldn't work.

And also, being dull isn't a good start for their chosen career.

Dull doesn't work in advertising.

As Bill Bernbach said: "Hard sell may not always drive out soft sell. But in advertising, as in life, the energetic always displaces the passive."

So I talked about energy, and being outrageous.

I talked about the fun and excitement of being outrageous.

The rush of doing something you're not supposed to do, and getting away with it.

I told them, for me, that's what great advertising was about.

All the people I really admired: Bill Bernbach, George Lois, Charlie Saatchi, Paul Arden, and Ed McCabe were the outrageous ones.

I asked them if they'd ever done anything outrageous.

One guy said he'd been expelled from school.

I asked what for.

He said he hated his teacher, and his teacher loved his tree.

So he'd burnt his tree down.

Well fair enough, that's outrageous, so it's a start point.

The problem is it doesn't really have a purpose.

It's undirected outrageousness.

Better to take that rebellious energy and put it to a purpose.

Like Andy McNab.

He was growing up to be a violent criminal in South London.

He says that if he hadn't found the army, and the SAS, he would certainly have ended up in prison.

But the special forces gave him a direction for that energy.

He stopped being violent for no reason.

He began to control it and it gave him two very successful careers.

One in the special forces, and one as an author.

So if we can find a natural rebelliousness within ourselves (and presumably that's why we went to art school), if we can harness that, we have an energy that we can turn into something useful.

Something exciting and different.

We can be outrageous to a purpose.

That, for me, is great advertising. ■

BE HERE NOW

I went to a gay wedding at a castle in Scotland recently.

The thing that struck me most was the ceremony.

They didn't go through the usual, "Do you take this man to love, honour, and obey…" which no one ever listens to or remembers.

Instead, each of them read out ten reasons why they loved the other person and wanted to spend their life with them.

Ten things they found about this person that made them unique.

That really struck me.

How many heterosexual couples have you heard put that much thought into why they're getting married?

How many married couples could even do that?

And yet, when we make that commitment, we're planning to spend our entire lives with that person.

After the ceremony I was talking to the Humanist minister.

She said she preferred same-sex weddings because people put more thought into them.

There wasn't an established routine they could slot into, so they had to really think about the purpose of what they were doing and why.

They couldn't go on autopilot, like everyone else.

And it reminded me of a quote from Pablo Casals.

"Every moment is a new and unique experience that will never come again. And what do we teach our children? That two and two makes four, and Paris is the capital of France."

We aspire to live on autopilot.

To find a formula and stick to it.

To defend it.

As if we were frightened of being alive.

There's a true Zen story that takes place two hundred years ago in Japan.

It was raining as the two leading Zen masters met to debate their different styles of teaching.

The first Zen master was seated drinking tea.

The second master entered and sat opposite him.

The first master said, "On which side of your shoes did you leave your umbrella?"

The second master paused, and realised he didn't know.

He immediately gave up being a master and became a pupil of the first Zen master.

By not knowing something as simple as that, he realised he had been thinking about the debate instead of actually being alive.

You see, the only time you can actually be alive is now.

And now is a very tiny point in time.

Now….it's gone.

Now….it's gone.

That's why we live most of our lives in the future or the past.

We worry about the future, and we regret the past.

But, of course, the future and the past don't actually exist.

Except as concepts in our mind.

So we live our lives, not out in the world, but in our minds.

That's what the Zen master realised he was doing.

Thinking about something else.

And while he was doing that he wasn't really alive.

So he went back to start learning to actually be alive, all over again.

Not to live in the future or the past.

To live in now.

But, in the real world, how many of us can live like that?

I only ever knew one person: John Webster.

In the morning he'd pick up a bunch of scripts and go through them as if he'd never seen them before.

He'd laugh out loud with surprise at a joke he'd written the day before.

John had no memory of what happened yesterday.

That freshness gave him an ability to see things the rest of us couldn't see.

He was living, and working, in the here and now.

So everything was always new and surprising.

The rest of us would get tired after a few days working on something.

John was always fresh as a daisy.

Every time he saw an idea was the first time he'd seen it.

So nothing was ever boring.

He was the advertising version of an absent-minded professor.

Graham Rose used to call him "a blithering genius".

His whole world consisted of whatever he was working on right now, and he was oblivious to any distractions.

He didn't waste his energy worrying about the past or future.

He spent all his energy on the now.

And I guess that's what real creativity is.

Energy.

And if we can be alive, here now, in this moment, there's opportunity, and surprise, and fun.

There's none of that if we're stuck in our mind, all there is is worrying about the future or the past.

And all that does is sap our energy. ■

DON'T OVER-THINK IT

It's amazing how your mind creates reality.

I once heard the script writer Frank Muir talking about the first time he went to New York.

He said he was terrified because he'd heard what a dangerous town it was.

As soon as he got off the plane at Kennedy airport he felt jumpy.

He kept looking over his shoulder, suspecting everyone.

But he managed to make it to a taxi without getting mugged.

All the way into Manhattan he was sure the cab driver was going to drive up a back alley where a gang was waiting.

But it didn't happen and he got to the hotel safely.

He made it from the cab to the hotel in one piece.

He checked into the hotel, got upstairs to his room and began to relax.

He looked out of his window at Central Park.

In the twilight it looked beautiful, sun setting behind the skyscrapers on the other side.

He was filled with a sense of just how great New York is.

He thought he'd been overreacting, he felt foolish.

He thought, "I can't be in one of the greatest cities in the world and hide in my hotel room."

So he decided to go for a walk.

He left the hotel and started walking along Fifth Avenue.

As he was looking up at all the tall buildings, a man bumped into him.

Then the man backed away, turned and walked off quickly.

Frank Muir thought, that didn't seem right.

He felt inside his coat and his wallet was gone.

He couldn't believe it, everything he thought about New York had been confirmed the minute he dropped his guard.

He yelled at the man and started running after him.

The man turned round, saw him coming, and took off.

Into the park.

Now the one thing you don't do in New York is go into the park after dark.

But Frank Muir was furious and he wasn't thinking properly.

He chased the guy into the park and caught him under one of the bridges.

He spun him around, slammed him against the wall, reached inside his coat and grabbed the wallet.

The man took off, running as fast as he could.

Frank Muir walked back to the hotel.

He thought, you don't have to be scared of New York, you just have to stand up for yourself.

Only weak people let themselves get taken advantage of.

He went up to his room feeling pretty pleased with himself.

And, when he opened the door to his room, he noticed his wallet was lying on the bed.

He hadn't taken it with him.

He looked at the wallet in his hand, the one he'd taken off the man, and saw it wasn't his.

He'd been so preconditioned, so petrified about New York that he realised what he'd done.

He'd chased an innocent man into the park and mugged him.

The other man was probably just another tourist like him.

Also petrified about being in New York and expecting to get mugged.

See, we think our mind interprets reality.

But actually our mind creates reality.

That's a pretty empowering thought.

All the things you thought were stopping you actually don't exist.

Unless you say they exist.

Then you make them exist and your behaviour reinforces them.

Sure objects exist, New York is there, that exists.

But as something to be terrified of it doesn't exist, unless you say it does.

If you decide to be terrified, then you will make it exist.

Once you know that, you are free to choose the reality that's going to make you empowered.

Rather than the one that's going to make you disempowered.

The one that's going to allow you to do the best work.

To fulfil your potential, whatever you decide that is.

Instead of the one that isn't.

You choose the reality.

Then you live it. ■

WE CAN'T GET A SPANNER ON IT

I've always found I've got most energy in the mornings.

So, if I'm really busy, that's when I like to work at home.

There are no distractions and it's usually more productive.

After about lunchtime I start to wind down a bit.

So that's a good time to go into the office and have any meetings.

A few years ago, I realised I'd left a script at home.

So I called home and spoke to our cockney cleaning lady.

I said, "Carol, can you see if there's a script lying on the dining room table?"

After a couple of minutes she found it.

I asked her to fax it to me.

She said she'd never used a fax machine.

So I talked her through feeding the paper into the machine, dialling the number and pressing send.

Then I went and stood by the office fax machine.

After a few minutes it rang and the script came out.

While I was checking it, the fax machine rang again.

And another script came out.

As I walked away it rang again, and another script came out.

Then it rang again, and another script came out.

I called home and a very flustered Carol answered.

I asked her what was going on.

She said, "Oh David I don't know what I'm doing wrong. I keep putting the script in, but it keeps coming out again."

See, technology is obvious once you know how it works.

But if you don't, it isn't.

I always remember my granny watching the early days of commercial TV.

She was watching a film and it ended and went straight into the adverts.

My granny carried on watching.

Then the News started with Big Ben striking.

Finally my granny looked up and said, "That was a bloody funny ending, wasn't it?"

Because no one told her they were adverts, she thought she was still watching the film.

She couldn't work out why some bloke had appeared from nowhere and what the chocolates had to do with anything.

Every generation understands their own technology.

When you grow up with something you accept it as the norm.

It's just part of your environment.

When new things appear later in life, you have to adapt and change.

And learning that way is harder.

I'm too lazy for that.

So any problems on the computer, anything that takes longer than two seconds to understand, I phone my son.

He usually logs on to my laptop, from wherever he is, and fixes it remotely on screen while I watch.

See I can't fix it because I can't get a spanner on it.

That's my generation.

He once asked me, "Dad, how come you don't understand computers?"

I said, "The same reason you don't know how a four-stroke engine works."

In my generation everything was mechanical.

Everything hit, pulled, turned or stopped something else.

Everything could be fixed by being tightened or loosened, filed or oiled.

Everything was logical.

Everything had a reason.

You could see how it worked and you could affect it directly.

So that governed our thinking, structure and reason, logic and argument.

Cause and effect.

This technology isn't like that.

You can't see why anything does anything.

You have to take it on trust, and that's governed everyone's thinking.

It's not about logic anymore.

That's dinosaur thinking.

It's about making things seem more complicated.

Not about making them simpler.

It's about feelings, and moods, and conversations, and engagement, and long words that no one quite understands fully, but you trust they work because they sound impressive.

Maybe that's what's wrong with advertising at the moment.

We can't get a spanner on it. ■

DRAWING WITH THE OTHER SIDE OF THE BRAIN

When I was about 17, I started doing A' level Art.

We weren't allowed to draw nudes at school.

So I signed up for the life drawing classes at East Ham Tech on Saturday mornings.

I had an image of life-class being about learning the structure of the human body.

So I thought we'd get fit, healthy specimens to draw.

I was the youngest person in the class, and eventually this grumpy, sixty-year-old naked model came and sat on a stool in front of us.

At first I wasn't sure if it was a man or a woman.

It had purple-dyed, bouffant hair like old ladies.

Plus makeup and sagging boobs.

But also a little posing pouch like a man would wear.

And a pot belly and stick-like arms and legs.

I was quite innocent, so I thought it must be a hermaphrodite.

It certainly wasn't one of the Greek gods and goddesses I'd expected.

Years later I found out that grumpy old model was Quentin Crisp.

The subject of the TV programme, 'The Naked Civil Servant'.

Sting even wrote a song about him, 'An Englishman in New York'.

But, at the time, I was just disappointed we didn't get a perfect body to draw.

Anyway, I realised if I was learning structure it didn't really matter what he looked like.

All the bones underneath were the same: arms, legs, head, hands, feet.

So I started to draw structurally: starting with the core balance line.

Usually one foot is taking all the weight: work out which one, then draw a straight upwards like an armature.

In a sculpture this would be the rod attached to the base, that everything else hangs off.

Then the directional lines for pelvis, ribs, chest shoulders.

Then relationship lines between ankles, knees, hands, elbows.

The same with the face: core tilt line for nose, directional lines for mouth, ears, eyes.

And I'd just keep building structures until a form appeared out of the mass of scaffolding.

That's how I've always drawn, structurally.

Many years later I married an art director and we had children.

When they were about 13 we decided it was time for them to start life classes.

So we booked up at a little art school in Hampstead, and on Saturday mornings, all four of us would go.

Then I noticed the way my wife drew was exactly opposite to me.

I started from the inside out, and drew structure.

By the time I'd got to the surface I wasn't really interested in the outside appearance.

So I started another drawing, investigating structure again.

My wife was exactly the opposite.

She wasn't interested in structure.

She started on the surface and drew in every detail, in perfect light and shade.

All her drawings looked almost photographically like the model.

I thought why is that?

Then I thought, probably because she's an art director and I'm a copywriter.

Art directors are right brain, copywriters are left brain.

Right brain is sensory and emotional.

Left brain is rational and logical.

Right brain arrives at a solution holistically and instinctively.

Left brain arrives at a solution incrementally by a process of deduction.

Which is how the best teams tend to work.

Copywriters work out what we're supposed to do, art directors come up with exciting ideas.

Art directors have flashes of inspiration, copywriters keep the whole process on track.

Which is also why they work better together.

Left to themselves, art directors would be exciting but wrong.

Copywriters would be right but dull.

I thought that was fascinating.

But then I would, I'm a copywriter so I'm left brain. ■

JUST BECAUSE YOU READ IT IN A BOOK DOESN'T MEAN IT'S TRUE

Ever heard the expression 'on your tod'?

It means to be, or do something, on your own, without help.

As in: "He stood guard all night, on his tod."

Ever wondered where it came from?

Well all you have to do is look it up in any of the various books on cockney rhyming slang.

There are several in Foyles.

All written by 30-ish middle class university graduates.

All of whom are experts in the derivation of cockney rhyming slang.

So to them, all slang must be rhyming slang.

Rhyming slang is where you leave the second part of the rhyme off.

So, if we go a bit Dick van Dyke for a moment, 'apples' means stairs, because the full rhyme is 'apples and pears'.

So in seeking the derivation of 'tod' they know it must be the first part of the rhyme.

And the second part must rhyme with (on your) 'own'.

So they'll tell you that 'on your tod' is believed to refer to a certain Todd Sloan, a man famous in the east end of London for riding around everyday, alone on his horse.

He liked to be alone.

Hence 'todd sloan' = alone.

Except that's bollocks.

These people assume that all slang is derived from rhyming slang because that's their preconception.

So they make the evidence fit their preconception.

The truth is 'on your tod' isn't rhyming slang at all.

I know, I was there.

It started with Elizabeth Taylor.

She married a Hollywood producer called Mike Todd.

He wanted to make the film 'Around The World In Eighty Days' starring David Niven.

It cost an absolute fortune and he couldn't get any backing.

At the time it was a famous story, how he scraped, and did whatever it took, to finance the film.

Against the odds he got it made, and it was a huge success.

In those days the biggest TV programme was 'Sunday Night At The London Palladium'.

The host at this particular time was Norman Vaughan.

He used to do a brief monologue at the beginning of the show.

One Sunday night he was grumbling that he'd had no help that evening.

"I've had to do everything on my Mike Todd," he said.

It got a huge laugh.

Because everyone knew what he meant without saying it.

The phrase 'on your Mike Todd' caught on.

Soon it got shortened to 'on your Todd' and eventually 'on your tod'.

And it passed into the language.

Now anyone who wasn't there at the time, to watch TV on that Sunday night, obviously won't remember that.

So they'll recreate it from the tools they've got.

And, as they say, if the only tool you've got is a hammer, every problem looks like a nail.

Or as Werner Heisenberg put it:

"What we observe is not nature itself, but nature exposed to our method of questioning."

It's the same way with ads as everything else.

We each have a preconception about what works and we can each put up a good argument.

Who wins?

Whoever makes the best argument.

But, as Tim Delaney once said to me, "Yes, but that doesn't make them right, just because they won the argument."

That's why an argument about ads is really kind of futile.

All that wins is the best argument, not necessarily the best ad.

Think of that next time you're on an awards jury, or with a client, or an account man or planner, or even your creative partner.

Someone might be better at arguing.

They might win the argument.

But they might still come up with the wrong answer. ■

BAD ARTISTS COPY, GREAT ARTISTS STEAL

Last week I heard an interesting programme on a Chicago radio station.

The famous copywriter Julian Koenig is still very upset that George Lois has taken credit for some ads he did in the 1960s.

These are 'Think Small' for Volkswagen, and 'If your Harvey Probber chair wobbles, straighten your floor'.

Both, really terrific ads.

Personally I've never seen George Lois's name anywhere near the VW ad.

Everyone knows that was Helmut Krone.

(The VW and Avis campaigns being the two most important case histories you learn when you start in advertising.)

But I have read several times George Lois taking credit for the Harvey Probber chair ad.

Lois says it was his idea and Koenig just changed some words.

Koenig, however, says Lois wasn't even in the room when he wrote the ad.

My attitude to these questions is always that you look at the track records of the people involved.

Who's done more great work?

For instance, supposing there are two guys.

One has been involved in dozens of great pieces of work with lots of different people.

The other guy has only been involved in one famous piece of work, and that's the one that's in dispute.

The weight of credibility has to favour the first guy.

So that has to be the focus of a career in this business.

Do as much great work as you can, with as many different people as you can, on as many different clients as you can, as fast as you can.

That way the weight of credibility is on your side.

You haven't just proved yourself in one situation, but over and over again.

Of course this means moving a lot faster and only dealing with the big picture.

If you spend your time worrying about details you have to go slower. Then you get bogged down.

There's a famous old Zen story about two monks walking alongside a river.

A woman is standing there crying.

The older monk asks what the problem is.

She says, "I need to cross the river, but if I do I'll ruin my kimono."

The older monk says, "Hop on my back."

And he carries her across, and puts her down.

The younger monk is furious, and for hours the two monks walk on in silence.

All day he rages inwardly, until at sunset he can't stand it anymore.

He turns to the older monk and says, "You broke the rule that says we aren't supposed to have anything to do with women."

The older monk says, "I left her at the river, you're still carrying her."

So I think the thing is, you might be right but what is it costing you?

While you're stuck with the detail you can't move on.

Everyone knows Julian Koenig was the writer on probably the most influential ad ever: Volkswagen's 'Think Small'.

Then he opened an ad agency with George Lois, called Papert, Koenig, Lois.

Then he and Lois split up, no one's heard much about him since.

After George Lois left that agency he set up another agency, called Lois Holland Callaway.

He did two decades of covers for Esquire that changed magazine covers for ever.

Today all magazine covers are still pale imitations of his originals.

He was involved in so many advertising campaigns, I can't even list them here.

And he was too full of ideas to be limited to just advertising.

He designed logos, restaurants, books, cars, interiors, anything he could get his hands on.

He's done at least ten times as much as the entire output of anyone else.

He's also probably a bully, and certainly an egotist.

So was Picasso.

If you go to the Musée Picasso in Paris, you'll see paintings by Van Gogh, Gauguin, Lautrec, Manet, Degas.

Except they aren't.

They're all by Picasso. While he was young and looking for his own style, he copied everyone.

Later he stole from everyone: Braque, Modigliani, Matisse, African art.

Until eventually it all came together to be Picasso.

One of the most prolific artists ever.

Julian Koenig's position is that George Lois was a better showman than an art director, and was better at promoting himself than he was at doing ads.

Well the same could be said of Picasso.

It's a fine line between charlatan and genius, even a blurred one.

You haven't got time to slow your life down to a speed at which you can gain everyone's approval for everything you do.

Do it, get on to the next thing.

Do it, get on to the next thing.

Do it, get on to the next thing.

After I'd left BMP someone called me up to say they understood John Webster had stolen some of my ideas, and they were having the same problem.

I said I didn't think John did any of that on purpose.

John was just so concentrated on whatever he was into he wasn't worried about details like that.

He was like an absent-minded professor.

He just took anything from anywhere to get the job done.

In fact sometimes he forgot and gave me credit for ideas he'd come up with.

So it worked both ways.

Ideas I'd come up with would never have seen the light of day without John.

I wouldn't even have recognised them as ideas without John.
So I got back ten times from John whatever he took.

I learned to forget the details and look at the big picture.
I'm not still carrying the woman.
I left her at the river. ■

HOW WORDS CLOUD OUR VISION

One of our art directors, Simone Micheli, was sitting opposite
me in the office, looking through The Art Direction Book.

Because he was opposite me, I was looking at the pages
upside-down.

Somehow the ads looked fresher, bolder.

One of them that particularly struck me, was an ad for TWA
that Neil Godfrey had done ages ago.

It had a plane in the middle distance, and a red carpet cutting
across half the white page in powerful perspective.

Apart from anything else, it was a just such a strong piece
of graphic design.

How come I never noticed that before?

Then it struck me.

It was because it was upside down.

So I couldn't read the words.

Normally I take a cursory glance at something then, within a
nanosecond, start to read it.

Once I'm involved in the words, the left side of my brain takes over.

The right side (the visual side) immediately gets put in second place.

That's why I was so much more impressed with the layout when it
was upside-down, and I couldn't read the words.

For the first time I was concentrating solely on the graphic qualities.

That's why Japanese art direction always looks so beautifully
designed to us.

Our brain isn't engaged in reading the words.

To us, there aren't any words.

The calligraphy is just another graphic element, so we're impressed with the design rather than getting sidetracked by the words.

This knocks on to semiotics.

The structuralist view is that we never actually see what we're looking at.

Rather we decode it for meaning.

So actually, language is the only reality.

All we ever see is symbols and concepts.

Symbols and concepts that exist only in our minds, not in reality.

I once read a book called 'Drawing With the Right Side Of Your Brain'.

At first I didn't get it.

I thought the right side was the visual side, so don't we always draw with the right side of our brains?

Apparently not.

We don't draw what we see, we draw symbols for what we know is there.

So, if I see a face, I start to draw the symbol that I know works for eyes.

A shallow curve for the top lid.

An inverted shallow curve for the bottom lid.

Similarly for lips.

A flattened-out letter 'M' for the top lip.

A flattened-out letter 'U' for the bottom lip.

And so on.

I draw symbols for what I know to be there rather than what I actually see.

I'm drawing in language: semiotics.

Which is how pretty much everything in the world works.

Road signs, packaging, clothing, cars, offices.

Everything is designed for the signals it gives off.

Everything is communicating, so everything is a language.

Mike Gold showed me a great way to prove the power of the left brain to override the right brain.

When I was making a speech, I had words printed on large cards in different colours.

I asked the audience, "Please shout out the colours the words are printed in, not the words themselves."

Then I'd hold up the word YELLOW printed in blue.

Then the word GREEN printed in red.

Then the word PINK printed in green.

Then the word BLUE printed in red.

In each case everyone shouted out the word, not the colour it was printed in.

Try it yourself.

Your mind reads the words aloud and steamrollers right over the colour your eyes actually see.

I noticed it again this morning.

I'd been through the Saturday paper, and bypassed all the ads without even noticing them.

Then I left the paper on the table.

My wife sat opposite me and started flicking through it.

And upside-down I started to actually notice all the ads I'd ignored.

When I couldn't read the words I started to appreciate the design.

Try it yourself.

See if it makes you think differently about how you do ads.

See if there's an opportunity there. ▪

THEORIES OF ACCOUNT HANDLING

There used to be a time when account men actually sold advertising to clients.

The theory was that the best advertising was brave advertising.

Advertising that stood out by breaking the category rules.

Given that the client had spent a long time learning and implementing the category rules, this was not an easy sell.

Every time you broke a rule the client would point out the 'mistake'.

The client needed someone to help them understand why you were breaking the rules.

Someone to hold their hand.

That was an account man's job.

I heard it put as follows:

"The client knows what he wants.

The agency knows what he needs.

The account man's job is to get the client to want what he needs."

Obviously every agency wants a happy client.

There are two ways to do this.

One: do the best job possible.

Two: do what the client wants.

They are the short-term view, and the long-term view.

In the short term the client will be happy if you do what he wants.

If it doesn't work, he won't be happy.

The alternative is you insist on doing what you believe to be right

In the short term the client may be unhappy.

But if it works, he'll be happy.

So the issue is: happy client in the short term, or the long term.

If you do what the client wants in the short term, and it doesn't work, you lose the account.

Likewise, if you do what you believe to be right, against the client's wishes, and it doesn't work you lose the account.

So, either way, you're betting the account on what you do working.

In short, you'll be left carrying the can.

So you might as well bet on the option you think will work.

Not just the easy option.

When I was at BMP I had a conversation with the (then) Head of Planning.

I thought the way we were using research made everyone lazy.

Instead of being a source of useful information, it became a thumbs up or down on whether work got made.

I thought we should use research findings as input, but still take the final decision ourselves.

One of the agencies I admired was Saatchi.

They'd always done disruptive work, long before the term 'disruption' was coined.

I thought the difference between them and us was the account men.

It wasn't that our creatives couldn't do work as daring as Saatchi, it was that our account men wouldn't sell it.

I said to the head of planning that I thought 'selling' had become a dirty word.

In his heavy Scottish accent he said, "So it should be. We're not some shyster outfit like Saatchi. We don't 'sell' work to a client. We lay the true facts of research before him and trust his own good sense and judgement to show him the correct path."

That's where we differed.

That's why I always thought one of the things that made Saatchi a great agency was Tim Bell.

An account man who actually sold work to clients.

That's also why I thought one of the things that made CDP a great agency was Frank Lowe.

Another account man who actually sold work to clients.

Apparently, CDP once had to present a long expensive commercial to a difficult client.

Frank went into the presentation and sat next to the client.

The account man played the commercial.

Frank and the client watched it together.

After the client had seen it, he said he wasn't sure about a particular part.

Frank said, "Do you know, that's exactly what I thought. I think we should see it again. Play it again for us please."

So the account man played it again.

Frank and the client watched carefully.

After it had finished, Frank patted the client's arm and said,

"No, I think we were wrong. It's actually okay."

And the client, reassured, bought it and ran it.

And that's how important real account men are.

We can have all the great ideas in the world, but if the account man doesn't get the client to run it, it'll never happen.

And all we've got is a bookful of great roughs. ■

THE BASIC BINARY BRIEF

Binary is a way of simplifying things down to their most basic.

This or that.

Black or white.

On or off.

No subtleties, just powerful, simple clarity.

Fast, easy decision.

Then quickly move on to the next fast, easy decision.

That's why computers work so fast.

Every decision is 0 or 1, that's it.

Is it possible for us to use that kind of brutal reductionism for what we do?

Yes of course.

The secret is how you organise the questions.

Don't ask everything at once.

Simplify it down so that's it's always one of two alternatives.

Then you can move through it really fast.

You'll sit in a briefing and hear,

"The brand obviously needs to grow share via trial, but still benefitting from market growth and capitalising on product benefits while maximising our brand values."

If that doesn't mean much to you, imagine how little it means to a consumer.

So we need to reduce everything down into a simple COMMUNICATION brief.

If it's going to be simple, we need to know 3 things:

WHO should buy it.

WHY should they buy it.

WHAT should they buy it instead of.

If we aren't clear on those 3 things, we can't put them in the ad.

If they're not in the ad, the consumer won't know.

If the consumer doesn't know, nothing happens.

So, learning from binary thinking, the first step is to accept that, at every stage, we can only do ONE thing properly.

So we have to reduce each stage to what that one thing is.

Question 1:

Brand Share or Market Growth.

Is your brand the market-leader or not?

Use the cola market as an example.

If you are Coca Cola you have way the biggest share of the cola market.

If you increase the number of people buying cola, you benefit much more than anyone else.

Whether consumers remember your name, or not.

If the market grows, you grow faster than anyone else, automatically.

But if you're not the market leader (Pepsi say) you don't want to do that.

You want to take sales from whoever is the market leader.

This gives you 2 very different sorts of communication briefs.

"Buy cola instead of other drinks."

(Market Growth, benefits Coca Cola).

"Buy Pepsi instead of Coke."

(Brand Share, benefits Pepsi).

Question 2:

Triallists or Current Users.

Do you want new people to try your brand?

(Essential for a launch.)

Or do you want current users to buy it more often?

Of course it depends on factors like market saturation.

Again, assume you were Coca Cola.

Pretty much everyone has tried Coke, so it's no good talking to triallists.

If you're Coke you have to tell current consumers why they should buy more.

So a communication brief could be, 'Have a coke with a friend'.

That way you sell two bottles instead of one.

But if you're Pepsi, and you're trying to take share from the market leader, obviously you need to tell Coke drinkers why they should try your brand.

So a communication brief could be, 'Pepsi tastes better than Coke'.

Question 3:

Product or Brand.

You could also refer to this as 'rational or emotional'.

Is there a definite, logical reason to purchase your product?

Or is there an emotional preference for the brand?

In the case of things you enjoy, it's usually an emotional preference for a brand: perfume, beer, fashion, confectionery.

No one cares much if those last longer, work better, or cost less.

They buy the imagery not the functionality.

In markets where all products are exactly like all other products, you do brand advertising.

But in other areas, facts can be more important: insurance, medicines, cars, technology.

People don't buy insurance on imagery, they buy it on cost.

Do you have a provable product benefit that no one else has: costs less, lowers cholesterol, works faster, lasts longer?

You need to have the discussion before you do the ads.

Sometimes Product (facts) can become Brand (image).

Mercedes, Volvo, VW, Sony, Tesco, Sainsbury, Apple.

All these brands did great factual advertising which built their brands.

Please remember, the Binary Brief is just a language, it's not a solution.

It's to enable creatives to have a back-and-forth discussion on the COMMUNICATION brief in simple words they can understand.

It's to force everyone involved to choose which ONE thing they want to say.

To force everyone to keep it simple, clear, and fast.

To force people to make uncomfortable decisions before the ads are written.

If we don't do that for the consumer they'll do it themselves.

The average person experiences nearly 1,000 advertising communications a day in their very busy lives.

Just like the binary, we're either on or off. ■

THE DIFFERENCE BETWEEN A CREATIVE PITCH AND A PITCH WITH CREATIVE WORK

Mike Gold had pretty much managed to talk London Transport Advertising into giving us their account.

He just had to take the client to lunch to finalise the details.

He said it would help if we could convince him of our design credentials.

Well one of the partners in our agency was Gordon Smith.

Gordon was a terrific art director.

So Goldie said Gordon should come along at the end of the meal for coffee, to meet the client.

So that's what happened:

Goldie and the client had a great lunch, everything was sorted.

Then, just as they were drinking coffee Gordon walked in.

The client looked up, saw Gordon, and said, "You?"

Gordon looked at the client and said, "You?"

And the client got up and stormed out.

Goldie was gobsmacked, he said, "What happened there?"

Gordon said, "You didn't tell me he was the client."

Goldie said, "Did you know him?"

Gordon said, "Yes, he used to be an account man at Vernons when I was an art director there."

Goldie said, "What happened?"

Gordon said, "Well we had a disagreement, and the last time I saw him I left him unconscious in a skip on Great Portland Street."

So that was the end of the London Transport Advertising account.

Sometimes pitches are like that, unpredictable.

One time we pitched for Hawaiian Tropic suntan lotion.

We did some really nice double-page spread press ads.

We were really pleased with the campaign.

Mike Gold said, "You can't show that, I've just done the media plan and it's 48 sheet posters."

I said, "You never told us."

Goldie said, "Well I'm telling you now, it's posters. You'll have to redo the creative work."

I said, "I'm telling you it's press. You redo the media plan."

But of course, he didn't and I didn't.

So at the pitch we all presented our work to the client.

The client said, "You've just shown me press ads, but the media plan is posters." I said, "We know. Creative and Media couldn't agree."

So that was the end of the Hawaiian Tropic account.

But one of the most creative pitches we did, didn't involve creative work at all. Mike Greenlees was pitching for Polyfilla, the DIY account.

Pollyfilla comes in a tub and it's for repairing cracks and holes in walls.

Mike wanted to brief us on creative work for the pitch.

I said we'd just done seven pitches and lost them all with creative work.

The way we were doing pitches, by showing creative work, wasn't working.

Maybe it was time to try something different.

He asked what I meant.

I said, "I think we should do a creative pitch. But without ads, with some pitch theatre instead."

Mike said that wasn't how we did it.

I said, "Well I'm not doing any ads, so we'll have to."

We had a huge row about it and Mike was so angry he kicked a hole in the wall. Then, on the day of the pitch he got a tub of Polyfilla and a trowel.

He said to the clients, "The problem with your current advertising is it makes everything look too easy. This makes Polyfilla look like it's not for serious jobs."

Then he got the trowel and started to put the Pollyfilla in the hole in the boardroom wall.

It fell out.

Mike said, "Look, that's what happens in the real world."

He put it back in again.

It fell out again.

Mike said, "See, it's not easy."

He put it back in again.

It fell out again.

Mike said, "It takes practice to get it right."

This time it stayed in.

He smoothed it off.

It looked like a good, professional job, and the clients applauded.

Mike had proved to them that we were an agency that understood DIY.

The clients left, very impressed.

Then, as they shut the door, the Pollyfilla fell out of the wall again.

It ruined the boardroom carpet.

But, by that time, Mike had already got the account.

Which proves you need a creative pitch to win an account.

But you don't always need creative work. ■

ADVERTISING AND SEX

A few years back, I read an article in The Spectator.

It was by Madsen Pirie, the chairman of The Adam Smith Institute.

He was writing about the phenomenon that, in the UK, girls were passing more exams than boys.

He was interested in the reason behind this.

Some people thought it was because more girls were being allowed to take exams at higher level.

Madsen Pirie said this wasn't the answer.

Some people thought it was proof that girls have always been more intelligent, but until now they hadn't been allowed to show it.

Madsen Pirie said this wasn't the answer either.

He said everyone was looking in the wrong place for the answer.

The reason girls were passing more exams than boys wasn't actually to do with girls' intelligence at all.

It was to do with the exams themselves.

At about the time when girls began passing more exams than boys, exams had changed.

The examination authorities had begun giving 50% of the marks for the course work, done in the year leading up to the exam.

Previously, 100% of the marks had been for the final exam itself.

Course work hadn't counted for anything.

This suited boys, who would do as little as possible all year, and cram like crazy in the last weeks before the exam.

Then it changed, and 50% of the marks were given for course work.

This suited girls, who would work steadily and conscientiously all year.

So that, by the time of the final exam, they would already have more marks than the boys.

And, however hard the boys crammed for the final exam, it was only worth 50% of the marks.

Madsen Pirie then interviewed a Cambridge don on the difference between male and female undergraduates.

He said that, generally speaking, the girls were better on the detail, but fuzzy on the big picture.

The boys were better on the big picture but sloppy on the detail.

He said his two best students were a male and a female, and they would both get 'firsts'.

How does this work in advertising terms?

Years ago Amanda Walsh, our CEO at the time, asked me why there were fewer women in the creative department than other departments.

She wanted to know if I thought it was just old fashioned sexism. I said I didn't think so.

The creative department is basically a big playground.

Lots of time spent telling jokes, playing games, reading comics or books, watching reels or YouTube, basically (what looks like) time-wasting.

None of this is a problem as long as, by the deadline, you've managed to turn it into a great idea.

Great ideas don't happen slowly, incrementally, and conscientiously.

They tend to happen as a result of a short, intense period of cramming information and then a sudden explosion of creativity. More the way boys approach exams than the way girls do. Account handling, on the other hand, requires exactly the opposite values.

Constant attention to detail, an intuitive ability to read situations and feelings, conscientious application that ensures everything possible has been done as it needs to be.

In short, the account handling department gives a lot more marks for course work than the creative department does. ■

MY FIRST ENCOUNTER WITH A PLANNER

My first encounter with a planner was at BMP in the seventies.
I'd just come back from New York, and they didn't have
planners there.

Over there the creatives had to do the thinking for themselves.
So I'd never met a planner before.

The first one I met (like every single planner I've ever met since)
had a university degree.

He also had a beard.

And glasses, roll neck jumper, corduroy trousers, and Earth Shoes
(the seventies version of Birkenstocks).

In fact, the whole university intellectual look at that time.

Anyway, we were working on Pepsi.

The target market was 13-year-old kids, and they were trying to
find out more about them.

So I sat behind a two-way mirror and watched this guy run
the group.

They were a scruffy little bunch of 13 year-olds from Poplar.

The planner pointed to a large board with the names of lots of
TV shows on it.

He said to the kids,

"Now, do you watch any of these shows on television?"

One little kid said,

"Yeah, we watch all of them. Except Star Trek, UFO and
Thunderbirds. We don't watch them."

All the other little kids agreed.

The planner stopped and said,

"Would you repeat that?"

The little kid said,

"Yeah, we watch all of them, except Star Trek, UFO and Thunderbirds. We don't watch them."

The planner looked towards the mirror, which he knew we were behind, and raised an eyebrow.

He turned back to the group of kids.

He said,

"So, does this mean that speculation about some vague technological future has no place in your everyday lives?"

The little kid said,

"No, they ain't on no more." ■

THE PUNTERS HAVEN'T READ THE BRIEF

When Frank Lowe was CEO of CDP, he asked Ron Collins to come into his office.

He said they needed something really special for a new client.

Frank said it had to be something really outstanding, something absolutely amazing.

Ron said, "Okay Frank, where's the brief?"

As Frank walked Ron to the door, he put his arm round his shoulder.

He said, "You don't need a brief Ron. I don't think a brief will help you."

I think Frank understood that sometimes a brief can actually get in the way.

It can actually harm the creative process.

Especially if what we're trying to do is bigger than just conventional advertising.

If we're trying to get into the language.

Competing against television programmes, films, the Internet, music.

None of those start with a brief.

They start when someone has an idea.

Someone thinks they'll write a book.

Someone else reads the book and thinks it'll make a great stage play.

Someone else sees the play and thinks it will make a great film.

Someone else sees the film and thinks it will make a great TV series.

In the case of all really great mass-market pieces of entertainment, the idea appears before the brief.

Of course we can't do that.

We can't have an idea about something and then go looking for a client to sell it to.

For us the opportunity to do advertising, the brief, comes before the idea.

So naturally we start from there.

This means that, over the years, briefs have become formulaic.

Worse than that, they've become documents that cannot be deviated from.

Before an account man, planner, or client looks at a piece of creative work they say, "Let's just remind ourselves of the brief first."

Why is this?

The consumer won't have read the brief before they're exposed to it.

So we're judging the work in exactly the way the consumer won't.

Why not experience it the way the consumer will?

Look at the work first.

Then you can ask yourself the really important questions about it.

Will it stand out?

Did I enjoy it?

Do I know who it's for?

Do I know what's it's saying?

When you've got those answers, then you can look at the brief.

Then you can see if the ad does what the brief says it's supposed to do.

Because, if you read the brief first, you're not judging what the ad does.

You're judging it against what it's supposed to do.

And here's a really shocking thought.

What if the final work was BETTER than the brief?

What if it's worth relooking at the brief in light of the work?

Because what will be judged by the consumers is the final work, not the brief.

But the brief has become the limits of creativity.

If the work doesn't tick all the boxes, we don't want it.

The brief was always supposed to be a springboard for great work. Not a straitjacket.

But about 75% of the creative opportunities have been taken away before the brief gets anywhere near the creative department.

The marketing strategy has been decided.

The communication strategy has been decided.

The research methodology has been decided.

The consumer insights have been decided.

The brand personality has been decided.

The proposition has been decided.

The media has been decided.

What does that leave the 'creative' department?

Words and pictures.

Oh yes, and they can pick a director.

There's really not much room left for any truly creative activity.

All that has been taken away and handled in a not very creative way.

What this leads to is departmentalisation and silo-thinking.

Real creativity happens when different people from different disciplines get together to overlap and have ideas about what each other does.

That's how we get fresh thinking.

We don't always have to use it, but it will help jog us out of our rut.

These are my personal rules for briefs:

1)   Read and sign off every brief before it goes into the creative department. Then forget it.

2)   Don't re-read the brief before you look at the work. Come to the work fresh.

3)   The wrong brief early is better than the right brief late. Often the original thinking is right, if it isn't you can always put a better brief in later.

Stay open to possibility.

The brief should be the floor, not the ceiling.

Mainly, lighten up.

This is supposed to be fun.

Fun in, fun out. ■

WHAT I LEARNED FROM MY MOTHER-IN-LAW

My mother-in-law is Singaporean Chinese.

She comes over to London to stay with us, and make a fuss of her grandchildren like all grandmas do.

A few years ago we were having the house renovated and she was watching the workmen putting in the drains.

She went out to take them a cup of tea.

She said, "Excuse me, I think you should put a cover on the manhole while you're working."

The workman said, "Sorry love?"

She said, "Otherwise you could get rubble in the drainage pipes and it could be a problem later on."

The workmen looked at each other.

They figured it was just an old Chinese lady getting confused.

They said, "Don't you worry love, we know what we're doing."

And they ignored her and carried on.

Six months later the drains started to back up and overflow.

They thought some of the bends in the pipes might have been too sharp.

So they dug them up and replaced them.

The system still didn't work.

They thought the angle of the drop might not have been steep enough for the flow.

So they dug down and raised part of it.

It still wasn't flowing properly. All the experts stood around and looked at it.

They sucked air through their teeth and scratched their chins.

They were out of ideas.

The only thing to do was put a CCTV camera down there.

Send it along the pipe and see if it could locate the problem.

This cost a lot of money, but eventually they located the source of the blockage.

Rubble.

The very same rubble that my mother-in-law had advised the workers about when they were putting the pipes in.

If they'd listened to her, and covered up the manhole, they wouldn't have had the problem.

And they'd have saved themselves a lot of time and money.

A little while later we were having a new shower fitted.

My mother-in-law took a cup of tea up to the workman putting it in.

She said to him, "Excuse me, is that a fibreglass shower tray?"

He said, "Yeah, probably."

She said, "Fibre glass is no good, you need a fired-clay shower tray."

He said, "Pardon?"

She said, "Fibre glass won't take the weight."

He looked at the little old Chinese lady and said, "Don't you worry love, I'll put a wooden frame under it."

He thought that would keep her quiet.

But my mother-in-law said, "The floors are also wood, and wood expands and contracts with heat. So, with summer and winter and hot and cold water, the basin will move and it will leak. If you are going to use a fibreglass shower tray you'll need a concrete base. Otherwise please put in a fired-clay shower tray which will take the weight and not move."

The guy went back and checked with his boss.

They checked with their suppliers.

And sure enough it should have been a fired-clay shower tray.

So they put it in and it hasn't leaked once.

What the workmen didn't know about my mother-in-law was that in Singapore she ran one of the largest plumbing companies, also a cast iron foundry, and a stainless steel works.

My father-in-law had built up these companies.

But because he didn't speak or write English, he needed her help to run them.

And, because she was better educated, she had to translate everything he wanted done.

He would want her to order large submersible pumps from Germany.

So she would need to know the pressure rating, the rpm, and the rate of fluid movement, etc.

He would want to order massive steel pipes from Australia.

So she would have to know the diameter, the connections, the lining, the rate of flex, etc.

Then she would negotiate contracts and tender for jobs.

She would also need to direct the workers on site, and at the factories, and check the quality of their work.

All the English workmen saw was a little old Chinese lady bringing them a cup of tea.

What they didn't see was a blue-collar trained, hands-on

specialist-plumbing contractor.

She had handled jobs larger than any of them had, for longer than any of them had been working.

In short, she had probably forgotten more than they would ever know.

But, because she didn't match their preconceptions, they didn't listen.

So they couldn't learn.

In our job, in advertising, we can't afford to be like that.

We deal in separating perception from reality. So we really need to be willing to learn.

We need to be on 'receive' not on 'broadcast'.

Life doesn't always fit our preconceptions.

And that's a problem if we're lazy.

If we come at everything with a preformed opinion, looking for the easy option.

In that case anything new and unusual is a problem.

Life is only an opportunity if we embrace newness and discovery.

If we enjoy finding out things that surprise us.

So that, when we do our job, we can surprise other people. ■

REASONABLE PEOPLE

I was listening to Dame Ellen MacArthur on Desert Island Discs.

She became the youngest person, ever.

To sail single-handedly.

Nonstop.

Around the world.

The interviewer asked her who were her inspirations.

She said, "My grandmother was very influential."

The interviewer asked why.

Ellen MacArthur said,

"She always wanted to go to university, and in fact she won a scholarship to pay for her to go. But her father, my great-grandfather, wouldn't allow her to go. They were a poor family, and he said she needed to get a job to bring money into the household. So she did, but later she made sure her three daughters went to university. And she was so fascinated with learning that every day, when I was young, she used to come to my school and sit in the canteen with me and my friends. Then, when she was old and retired, and at the end of her life, she went back to university to get a degree. And she finally graduated three months before she died."

So there's a clue to where Ellen MacArthur got the determination that made her sail a ship, that should have been crewed by a dozen men, for 71 days.

Alone.

Thousands of miles from anywhere.

The nearest land 7 miles straight down.

The waves twice as high as the average house.

Sleeping a few minutes at a time, always on deck.

The interviewer asked her about her first boat.

How did she get it?

She said it was a little, tiny dinghy and she saved up for it.

"We didn't get any pocket money when we were little. So, anything
we wanted, we either had to make it or save up for it. I used to
save the change from my school-dinner money every day."

The interviewer asked her to elaborate.

She said, "Every day I'd eat beans, mashed-potato, and gravy.
Beans cost four pence, mashed potato cost four pence, gravy
was free. So I'd have the beans and mash swimming in gravy, almost
like soup. Everyone thought I was crazy. But I'd go home and stack
the change up next to my savings tin. When the change reached £1,
I'd put it in my savings tin. Then I'd fill in one of the little squares on
a sheet of graph paper I had on the wall. When I had 100 little
squares filled in I'd take the money to the building society."

The interviewer asked her how much her first boat cost.

She said, "£535".

And you get another clue to the level of determination she
considered normal.

The interviewer then asked what life had been like at home.

She said she'd been very happy at home, if slightly unconventional.

The interviewer asked her for an example.

She said, "Well, I only had a very small bedroom. There really wasn't
room in it for the bed plus everything else I was making and storing.
So when my parents went out one day, I took the bed apart and

put it in the barn. I figured, if I asked them, they were likely to object. But if I did it while they were out it would be a fait accompli. And from then on, I just slept on the floor in a sleeping bag, and had lots more room for everything I wanted to do in my bedroom."

You get another clue to the sort of determination that could make her climb to the top of a mast six stories high.

On her own in the middle of the ocean.

With the ship speeding along at forty miles an hour in the pitch dark.

And fix a broken block-and-tackle in sub-zero temperature.

You see, none of what she did was reasonable behaviour.

Not saving £500 from her lunch money.

Not throwing her bed out of her bedroom.

Not sailing single-handedly, non-stop, around the world.

Not for a 19-year-old.

Not for a woman.

What I loved about listening to her was that she didn't let other people's ideas of what was reasonable dictate her behaviour.

She looked at the problem.

Worked out what she thought was the best way of proceeding.

Then, if it made sense to her, she went ahead and did it.

Whatever anyone else said.

She didn't let other people's version of what was reasonable stop her.

She came to her own conclusion.

How many of us do that?

How many of us question what we're told and come to our own conclusions?

Don't we usually just do what we're told?

Reasonable people don't do what she did.

Not the big things, not even the little things.

Because reasonable people just want to fit in.

So they don't question what other people tell them.

But then reasonable people don't do much. ■

DON'T TRUST ANYONE

Jack Charlton was Bobby Charlton's big brother.

Bobby Charlton is considered one of the best English footballers of all time.

When Pele put together his team of all-time greats, Bobby Charlton and Bobby Moore were the only Englishmen on it.

Even foreign waiters who didn't speak English could all say one phrase, "Bob-bee Charl-ton."

Usually said smiling and nodding, with the thumbs up.

He was a sportsman and a gentleman.

An advocate of fair play and a credit to the game.

His big brother Jack wasn't like that.

'Big' Jack Charlton was a pragmatist.

At Leeds, he pretty much invented the professional foul.

The penalty-kick was designed to stop defenders fouling opposing players in front of the goal.

Everyone avoided giving away a penalty.

It was bad sportsmanship

But Jack Charlton thought it made sense.

If they looked certain to score bring them down.

Kick 'em, grab their shirt, the ref might not see and you might get away with it.

Even if they got a penalty, they might not score from the spot.

It made sense, it was pragmatic.

Jack Charlton knew he wasn't as good as his little brother Bobby.

He couldn't depend on his ability.

So he had to use his brains.

And his shoulders, his elbows, and his knees, backing into forwards as they jump.

Whatever it takes.

Whenever Leeds would play Manchester United, Big Jack used to get a phone call from their mum before every game.

She'd say, "Hey you, leave our kid alone. Don't go kicking lumps out of him again, alright."

Up against his brother Jack, even one of the best players in the world, Bobby Charlton, needed his mum to defend him.

Jack Charlton knew he was the underdog.

That meant he had to use anything and everything to stand any chance at all.

When he became manager of Middlesborough he taught his players to think like underdogs.

We're not as good as the rest, so use anything and everything to beat them.

It was said that his players would "run through walls" for him.

Middlesborough was a feared team when Big Jack was in charge.

When it became vacant, he applied for the job of England manager.

The FA didn't even reply to his letter.

He wasn't their sort of chap.

Too rough, too crude, questionable methods.

They gave the job to someone much nicer, a gentleman.

And England didn't even qualify.

But Ireland weren't so sniffy.

They got Jack Charlton to manage their team.

And Big Jack brought his brand of thinking to the job.

Ireland usually didn't make it to the World Cup.

The country was too small, too few players to choose from.

But Big Jack did what he always did.

He questioned conventional wisdom.

He didn't take anything on trust.

He started from scratch and re-read the rules.

He found you didn't actually have to be born in a country to play for that country.

You just had to have one grandparent from that country.

Suddenly a light bulb went on in Jack's head.

Pretty much everyone in England has an Irish granny.

That meant he now had virtually every English player to choose from as well as every Irish one.

So Big Jack put his team together.

That year Ireland qualified for the world cup.

And more than that, they beat Italy, one of the best teams in the world.

England fans had to sit at home and watch it on the telly.

Because, thanks to the FA, England didn't even qualify.

Jack Charlton didn't accept whatver brief he was given.

He knew he couldn't afford to be complacent.

So he behaved like the underdog.

He got creative.

He questioned the brief.

How often do you find yourself in that situation?

You're given a bad brief, and told not question it.

The planners have asked all the questions.

The account men know all the answers.

The client doesn't want any input thanks.

Think of Big Jack.

Don't moan about it.

Find a way to change it.

Jack Charlton was in the England team that won the World Cup in 1966.

He said to the manager Alf Ramsey, "I'm not one of the best players in the country, how come you picked me?"

Alf Ramsey said, "Because you don't trust Bobby Moore."

Bobby Moore was one of the best players in the world, and Jack Charlton didn't trust him.

So he covered his every move in case he did something stupid and lost the ball.

Jack Charlton played on a great World Cup team.

And he built and managed a great World Cup team.

Three lessons about creativity from Big Jack.

Don't trust anyone to do your thinking for you.

Don't accept that the brief can't be changed.

Always believe you're the underdog. ■

THE NEW BUSINESS DILEMMA

Suppose you are a doctor.

A man comes to see you and he's limping, you examine him.

You say, "It's an easy diagnosis, you've got a broken leg."

He says, "I don't want a broken leg."

You say, "That's understandable, but you still have a broken leg."

He says, "I'm the patient and I don't think I've got a broken leg. I think I've got a sprained ankle."

You say, "Well I'm the doctor. I've seen lots of these, and you've got a broken leg."

He says, "You may be the doctor, but it's my body and I think I know it better than you. So when I say I've got a sprained ankle, that's what I've got."

You say, "Of course you know your body, but you're not an expert in medicine. I am, and I say you've got a broken leg."

He says, "Well I've told you the problem I want fixed. Now you can either fix it for me, or I can go down the road to another doctor and pay him to fix my sprained ankle."

What do you do?

Lose the patient, or give him the wrong treatment?

If you're in advertising, you treat him for a sprained ankle and take the money.

Because the first rule is to keep the client happy.

Obviously you don't want to lose the client.

There's an expression in American basketball, "You can't shoot the ball if you ain't got the ball."

And that's how it is in advertising.

You can't do any great work unless you have the account.

So you do whatever it takes to win the account.

Otherwise you're stuck with the Benn/Kinnock dilemma.

Tony Benn was a very principled left wing politician.

He was originally Anthony Wedgwood Benn, Viscount Stansgate.

But he believed deeply in the principles of socialism.

So he helped pass a law that allowed him to become the first person ever to renounce a peerage.

He renounced it all and changed his name to Tony Benn.

The trouble is, real socialism is a bit too extreme for most people.

And political parties have to sacrifice a lot of their more extreme principles to become electable.

Neil Kinnock understood that very well.

When he became leader of the Labour party, he set about reforming it.

Watering down or getting rid of some of the more fundamental socialist principles it had been founded on.

Principles he thought stopped it achieving power.

Benn and Kinnock had a massive row over these reforms.

Benn said to Kinnock, "You'll just have power without principles."

Kinnock said to Benn, "That's better than principles without power."

Well is it, what do you think?

Maybe it depends where you come from, your background.

Kinnock came from a poor family in Wales.

When you're poor the most important thing is survival.

Tony Benn had been brought up in the lap of luxury, survival was never even an issue.

So, because survival was assured, principles became the most important thing.

During the cold war there was a serious risk of nuclear annihilation.

One Russian bomb could destroy London.

In the USA and Europe you'd often hear the phrase repeated, "It's better to be red than dead."

No one wanted to be communist, but if you had to choose which would you choose?

It's a more extreme version of the advertising dilemma.

Do you try to win new business by giving the client what you know he wants?

Or do you give him the right answer even though you know he doesn't want it?

As Bill Bernbach said, "A principle isn't a principle until it costs you money."

It's the Kinnock/Benn dilemma.

We need to find a way to pick our way through the two extremes.

In the old days Saatchi had a rule of thumb for whether they accepted business or not:

"We've either got to be doing great work on a piece of business, or we've got to be making money on it. If we're not doing either of those, we don't want it."

That may not be the ideal solution.

It probably isn't the only solution.

But it is a good pragmatic route through the dilemma. ■

IT'S BETTER THAN REAL, IT'S FAKE

Kenwood House in North London is impressive.

The exterior, the interior, and the gardens.

As you approach you notice the perfect symmetry of the house.

Both wings match exactly, windows delicately balancing each other either side of the entrance.

Once inside, you're impressed by the library.

Both the extensive collection of books and the large marble pillars.

Looking out over the grounds you're impressed by the almost perfect view.

A Constable-style landscape gently rolling down to a meandering stream, disappearing under a wooden bridge.

It all seems too perfect to be real.

And it is.

It's all fake.

A huge, beautiful, elegant, impressive fake.

Robert Adam did the house, in the late 18th century.

Capability Brown did the gardens.

Take the beautiful marble pillars in the library.

They're actually made from wood, and painted to look exactly like carved white marble.

There are no books in the impressive library either.

Just the spines stuck to the wall.

The beautifully symmetrical windows are complete fakes on one side.

Stuck to the outside wall of the music room, which requires solid brick walls for its acoustic qualities.

The beautiful view of the gardens is worth investigating.

When you walk down to the stream it's actually two ponds and, on the left, the cut-out shape of a bridge stuck next to them.

A clump of trees between the ponds connects them in your eye, and the 'bridge' confirms the direction the 'stream' goes in.

The whole of Kenwood house is an exercise in trickery and manipulation.

The late 18th century was the height of The Enlightenment.

The Enlightenment was born out of The Reformation.

The idea that man wasn't just a slave to fear and superstition anymore.

For the first time, with reason and logic, man was able to work out and control his own destiny.

And Trompe L'Oeil was a visual manifestation of that.

Trompe L'Oeil just means 'trick the eye', what we'd call an illusion.

It became very fashionable in the late 18th century.

A way to demonstrate that the eye, and consequently the mind, could easily be fooled and manipulated.

Our senses couldn't be trusted.

We needed to stop 'believing' in things and make the effort to think for ourselves.

This is what separated the cultured individual from the merely wealthy.

Previously, a person's worth was based on wealth.

If you wanted a beautiful house, you just built it.

And the cost demonstrated how rich you were.

The Enlightenment signalled a change from money as the main indication of someone's worth.

Now intelligence was a much higher value.

Intelligence was demonstrated by an understanding, for the first time, of the mind's importance.

That the mind actually in fact determined reality.

Trompe L'Oeil was a visual manifestation of this.

If you trick the eye you trick the mind.

This was far cleverer than merely spending money on something that just looked like what it was.

How dull.

How wasteful.

It was better to use your brains rather than just throw money at it.

Far more clever to out-think someone rather than just out-spend them.

Take a look around at the advertising we're doing today.

Where million pound commercials are no longer anything unusual.

Where people brag in print that their commercial is the most expensive commercial ever filmed.

Do we think advertising could learn anything from Robert Adam and Capability Brown?

From Trompe L'Oeil and The Age Of Enlightenment?

Anything? ■

ROCK LOGIC vs WATER LOGIC

A rock is very strong.

It doesn't move.

It sits there being strong and immovable and right.

That's how rock logic works.

Water isn't strong, it's weak.

But what seems like a disadvantage is actually an advantage.

Water doesn't fight rocks, it goes around them.

It's always moving and exploring.

Trying everything, never getting stuck.

That's how water logic works.

Water logic is smarter than rock logic.

If a problem crops up, don't fight it head on like a rock.

Go around it like water.

Don't let it stop you, keep moving.

Going into areas where you'll discover things you don't know yet.

Try everything, even if you don't know where it's going to lead.

That's what water does.

It keeps flowing.

What can you do beside advertising?

Music, writing, sport, film, whatever.

Explore it and see what ways you can use it.

Adam Morgan was a planner at TBWA.

One day he made a list of all the famous people he'd love to talk to.

It was a long impressive list of people from all sorts of different fields.

Then he noticed they all had one thing in common.

They'd all challenged the status quo in their various fields.

Adam decided he could make this the thesis for a book.

And it would give him the excuse to interview all his heroes.

So he spent 6 months interviewing people and, at the end of it, he had a book.

It's called EATING THE BIG FISH.

It's the book that launched the concept of 'Challenger Brands'.

Just about every client, everywhere has read it.

Adam doesn't work as a planner at TBWA anymore.

He now has offices all over the world, working for clients who want him to run Challenger-Brand workshops for their companies.

Adam is an example of water logic.

Simon Veksner is a copywriter at BBH.

He's done a lot of really nice ads and won quite a few awards.

He also likes an argument, he likes to create controversy.

And he tapped into the fact that there were lots of people in advertising who also like to argue and sound off, and there was nowhere for them to do it.

So he created one of the most visited advertising blogs anywhere.

Most blogs are lucky to get 3 or 4 comments a week.

His blog routinely got a minimum 30 or 40 a day, usually more.

People all over the world clicked onto it: SCAMP.

His blog was picked up by Campaign and the trade press.

Which increased the number of people reading his blog.

Which meant the trade press had to check it regularly, and so on.

He created a virtuous circle.

All by looking to see where his energy was, and following it.

Scamp was another example of water logic.

Peter Souter was ECD at Abbott Mead.

That should be enough for anyone, right?

But Peter has always loved writing witty dialogue.

So he wrote a radio play, just because it interested him.

It was so well received he wrote a whole series of radio plays.

Which lead to him being offered a 10 part television series.

Which will probably lead to Hollywood. Impossible?

It wasn't for Al Parker when he was a copywriter at CDP.

He started making rough test commercials in their basement,
on an old video camera.

Just out of curiousity, initially.

Then he found out he enjoyed it.

So he moved into directing commercials.

He was so successful he wrote and directed a film: Bugsy Malone.

Then Hollywood: Midnight Express, The Commitments, Pink Floyd:
The Wall, Evita, and more.

Now he's Sir Alan Parker, knighted for his services to the British
film industry.

Paul Arden was ECD of Saatchis.

He wanted to write a book, but he was an art director,
not a writer.

So he put together a book for people who preferred pictures
to words.

It became one of the biggest-selling books in the world.

But you're probably saying, "That's all very well for them. But I'm
not as talented or driven as those famous, powerful people."

Well, when I was at BMP, there was an account man who loved photography.

He dreamed of a career as a photographer.

No one took him seriously.

He began going on safari holidays, and taking his camera, and sending the shots to wildlife magazines.

Years later, when I met him, he was a staff photographer for National Geographic.

They would send him all over the world on assignments.

And he now has his own massively successful online photo library of all the shots he's ever taken anywhere.

Rock logic is: stay where you're at and don't move.

Water logic is: try everything, see where it goes.

Just because you can't see the immediate short-term benefit of something, doesn't mean you shouldn't try it.

As we used to say in the playground, "Use it or lose it." ■

GLOSSARY

Anna & Elaine: (Micheli & Jones) Brilliant young all-girl creative team. Original, workaholic, very competitive.

AMV: Abbott Mead Vickers. Founded by David Abbott, Peter Mead and Adrian Vickers

Paul Arden: Enfant Terrible art director. Creative Director of Saatchi at its best, brilliant film director, author, you name it. Legend for a generation of advertising creatives.

ASA: Advertising Standards Authority: advertising censorship group.

BACC: Broadcast Advertising Clearance Centre. Nowadays known as Clearcast.

BBH: Bartle Bogle Hegarty: consistently the best UK ad agency over the past two decades.

Tim Bell: Now Lord Bell. Was CEO of Saatchi & Saatchi. Advisor to Maggie Thatcher. One of the best account men in UK advertising.

BMP: Advertising agency, Boase Massimi Pollitt. The great TV agency of the 1970s.

CDP: Collett Dickinson Pearce. The best British agency of the 60s and 70s. In its day the best in the world.

Murray Chick: Partner in the agency WTCS. Brilliant advertising planner, strategist and thinker.

D&AD: Design and Art Direction Association. The most influential advertising awards in the UK, possibly in the world.

GGT: Gold Greenlees Trott. Advertising agency, very influential in the 1980s.

Mike Greenlees: CEO of GGT. Brilliant account man, workaholic, team leader, pragmatist.

Tony Kaye: Unpredictable, mercurial, brilliant film and TV commercials director.

Frank Lowe: Now Sir Frank Lowe. Was CEO of CDP, the man who led it during its greatest years. Massive influence in UK advertising.

MCBD: Advertising agency:
Miles Calcraft Briginshaw Duffy

Graham Rose: Funniest man in advertising. Talented art director now an excellent commercials director.

Saatchi: Saatchi & Saatchi. During the 80s the biggest, and the best, advertising agency group in the world.

Scamp: Was advertising's largest blog. Worldwide audience, mainly grumpy youngsters with a chip on both shoulders.

Peter Souter: Witty and urbane ex-Executive Creative Director of AMV BBDO. Writes radio plays and TV series, probably films too by now. Advertising's Richard Curtis.

Ridley Scott: Now Sir Ridley Scott. The man who revolutionised the look of UK TV commercials. Now one of the most powerful directors in Hollywood.

Gordon Smith: Brilliant art director. Helped found GGT and BST. The 'S' in WTCS and now CST The Gate.

TBWA: Tragos, Bonnard, Wiesendanger & Arjoldi (well you asked). Massive international ad agency network.

David Thorpe: Brilliant advertising photographer. Photographic books include 'Rude Food' and 'Vin Rude'.

Amanda Walsh: Very powerful female 'suit'. MD ran WTCS. Great team leader.

WCRS: Wight Collins Rutherford Scott. Great ad agency founded by three great creatives and a very clever money man.

WTCS: Walsh Trott Chick Smith. My third agency, founded with a powerful account (wo)man, brilliant planner, and terrific art director.

Y&R: Young & Rubicam. Massive establishment American agency, merged in London to form Rainey Kelly Campbell Roalfe Y&R.

FINALLY, ROLL THE CREDITS

I really should say thank you to the people who helped, in fact forced, me to get this together.

David Greene, the publisher, is like a sergeant.
He organised the printers, the costs, the shipping, the publishing.
Nothing's a problem to David.
He just makes things happen and, like all effective people, can't understand why everybody can't do it.
Caroline Greene is the editor.
She told me what was missing and what was needed.
And she explained to me why what I had written was good, and why it was worth putting into a book.
Jade Trott is my daughter, she's an art director.
Lee Trott is my son, he's a copywriter.
They checked absolutely every word of everything I wrote before I let anyone else see it.
For the first time in their lives they got to be my boss.
They were my creative directors.
Cathy Heng is my wife, she art directed the book.
Every night, when I went to bed around midnight, Cathy stayed up until around two on the Mac, fussing with every page.
Doing and redoing the cover, the typeface, the layout, every miniscule aspect.
Without Cathy there wouldn't be a book.

There'd be a lot of typed-up pages stapled together.

Stevie Spring, CEO of Future Publishing, bullied me to start writing in the first place.

Without Stevie nagging me these would still just be funny anecdotes I tell over a drink or three.

And of course, my sister Shirley Cox, Executive Director of The Chemotherapy Foundation in New York.

Without her I wouldn't have gone to art school in New York.

So I wouldn't even be in advertising, much less writing anything.

Shirley was the big sister who could see things in her little brother that no one else could.

Without her I wouldn't have a career, much less a book.

There are lots of other great people in these stories.

But these are the ones who are mainly responsible for making it happen. ■